INSIGHT ⊙ GUIDES

EXPLORE

CUBA

◎ Walking Eye App

YOUR FREE EBOOK AVAILABLE THROUGH THE WALKING EYE APP

Your guide now includes a free eBook to your chosen destination, for the same great price as before. Simply download the Walking Eye App from the App Store or Google Play to access your free eBook.

HOW THE WALKING EYE APP WORKS

Through the Walking Eye App, you can purchase a range of eBooks and destination content. However, when you buy this book, you can download the corresponding eBook for free. Just see below in the grey panel where to find your free content and then scan the QR code at the bottom of this page.

Destinations: Download essential destination content featuring recommended sights and attractions, restaurants, hotels and an A–Z of practical information, all available for purchase.

Ships: Interested in ship reviews? Find independent reviews of river and ocean ships in this section, all available for purchase.

eBooks: You can download your free accompanying digital version of this guide here. You will also find a whole range of other eBooks, all available for purchase.

Free access to travel-related blog articles about different destinations, updated on a daily basis.

HOW THE EBOOKS WORK

The eBooks are provided in EPUB file format. Please note that you will need an eBook reader installed on your device to open the file. Many devices come with this as standard, but you may still need to install one manually from Google Play.

The eBook content is identical to the content in the printed guide.

HOW TO DOWNLOAD THE WALKING EYE APP

1. Download the Walking Eye App from the App Store or Google Play.
2. Open the app and select the scanning function from the main menu.
3. Scan the QR code on this page – you will then be asked a security question to verify ownership of the book.
4. Once this has been verified, you will see your eBook in the purchased ebook section, where you will be able to download it.

Other destination apps and eBooks are available for purchase separately or are free with the purchase of the Insight Guide book.

CONTENTS

Introduction

Directory

Credits

Best Routes

ART LOVERS

Havana (routes 1 and 2) and Camagüey (route 10) both have art galleries, studios, and street art installations to delight anyone seeking contemporary Cuban art.

RECOMMENDED ROUTES FOR...

BACK TO NATURE

Head to the protected forests and mountains of the Sierra Maestra (route 11), Sierra del Rosario (route 3), or Topes de Collantes (route 7) for a tropical natural wonderland.

BEACH ENTHUSIASTS

Cuba's northern cays (route 9) have the best sand, but more intimate beaches are found around Baracoa (route 13) while the Bay of Pigs (route 5) fascinates divers and snorkelers.

BIRDWATCHING

The Zapata peninsula (route 5) is essential for viewing endemic and migratory birds, while the national bird, the tocororo, can be seen in the mountains (routes 3 and 11).

ESCAPING THE CROWDS

Off the beaten track – visit the Jardín Botánico Soledad outside Cienfuegos (route 6) or hike to Playa Las Gaviotas on Cayo Santa María (route 9), a pristine, undeveloped beach.

HISTORY BUFFS

Cuba's 500-year history of struggle against oppression is showcased in the museums and plazas of Havana (routes 1 and 2), Santa Clara (route 8), Santiago de Cuba (route 12), and Camagüey (route 10).

MUSIC LOVERS

Cuban music can be heard everywhere but the best bars and clubs are in Havana (particularly Vedado; route 2), Trinidad (route 7), and Santiago de Cuba (route 12).

VIEWS

Nothing beats the *mogotes* and tobacco fields of Viñales (route 4), but the Valley of the Sugar Mills from the Manaca-Iznaga tower (route 7) is stunning, as is Havana from the 33rd-floor bar of Edif Focsa (route 2).

INTRODUCTION

An introduction to Cuba's geography, customs, and culture,
plus illuminating background information on cuisine, history,
and what to do when you're there.

Old Chevrolet car, Trinidad

EXPLORE CUBA

Cuba's varied natural beauty from mountain top to sea shore, its troubled history, elegant architecture, creative arts, and vibrant music and dance, combine to make this a fascinating, colorful, and exciting island.

Cuba inspires emotion. This, the largest of the Caribbean islands, thrills the senses, befuddles the mind and tugs at the heart. It is a place of magic and romance, where the sun lights up the colors of the day and music and rum fill the night. Cubans are lively and warm, expressive, and affectionate. They follow ballet, baseball, and boxing; their children have more rhythm in their little fingers than most tourists acquire in a lifetime.

Drawn from many continents over several centuries with migrants mainly from Africa, Spain, and China, Cubans have created a culture which has influenced artists and musicians worldwide, yet this was achieved despite the isolation of the island after the 1959 Revolution and the US trade embargo since the 1960s.

Tourism is bringing an end to Cuba's isolation as the country struggles to earn its keep. Cays where Hemingway fished undisturbed now host modern beach resorts along the formerly empty swathes of sand. Colonial mansions have been converted into boutique city hotels or museums. Tourists, however, are shielded from the harsh realities of life on the island, only rarely witness-ing the blackouts, the fuel and water shortages, the inadequate food rations, the long lines, leaky roofs, and heavy-handed bureaucracy that are the daily hardships for the average Cuban.

GEOGRAPHY AND LAYOUT

Variously described as a long, green alligator, or cigar-shaped, Cuba is much longer than people realise: 776 miles (1,250 km) from tip to tail, while 535 miles (861 km) of road separate the two main cities, Havana and Santiago de Cuba. While much of the island is flat or has rolling hills suitable for cyclists, there are three main mountain ranges: the Cordillera de Guaniguanico in the west, divided into the Sierra de los Organos and the Sierra del Rosario, the Sierra Escambray in the central area, and the Sierra Maestra in the east. Known as the Oriente, the east contains the highest peaks, with Pico Turquino rising to 6,476 ft (1,974 m).

A single road runs nearly the length of the island, with roads leading off it to major towns and coastal resorts. This road, the *autopista*, is poorly maintained and hazardous, being used by trucks,

Street art

Satue of Independence hero Antonio Maceo, Santiago

long-distance buses, cars, bicycles, and even horses and carts, while oxen and cowboys use the hard shoulder and grassy banks. On minor roads, signposting is poor to non-existent, often bleached by the sun, so get the best road map you can find if driving yourself.

Although there are international airports dotted around the island to help tourists reach their beach resorts as quickly as possible, many people still start their journey in Havana, which is where our routes begin, heading west to Viñales (route 4) by car, taxi or bus before setting off towards the east. While some places, such as Las Terrazas and Soroa on route 3 can be done as day trips out of the capital, it is assumed that a more leisurely pace with overnight stops is preferable for the routes further afield.

HISTORY

Not a great deal is known about Cuba's early settlers, although they are believed to have been pre-agricultural, pre-ceramic, hunter-gatherers who traveled from the Orinoco delta of modern-day Venezuela, from Central America and possibly also from Florida and the Mississippi basin some 6,000 years ago. From about AD 600 onward, these groups were gradually displaced by waves of more advanced immigrants, the Arawak-speaking Taínos, who made their way along the arc of Caribbean islands by means of canoes made out of hollowed-out tree trunks. The Taínos were farmers as well as hunters and fishermen, growing staple crops such as cassava, peppers, beans, sweet potatoes, guavas, and pineapple, as well as tobacco.

Christopher Columbus landed in eastern Cuba on 27 October 1492, but the Spanish didn't settle until Diego Velázquez arrived in 1511 with some 300 conquistadors. He founded seven towns, enslaved the Taínos and in the process exposed them to European diseases. Through sickness and mass suicide, their population fell from 150,000 to just 3,000 by the mid-16th century.

The arrival of the Spanish marked the beginning of turbulence and strife. The first settlers were frequently attacked by pirates and life was insecure. It was not until the 18th century that plantation agriculture brought untold wealth to the island and hundreds of thousands of African slaves were imported to grow and harvest sugar. By the middle of the 19th century Cuba produced a third of the world's sugar. There was little peace however, with the struggle for independence from Spain leading to wars and mass slaughter.

Independence was achieved with the help of the United States but with strings attached. In the first half of the 20th century, the US dominated the Cuban economy and its political processes. The disparity in incomes widened as corruption and violence increased under the strongman, General Fulgencio Batista. Millionaires flourished while

Trinidad schoolchildren

malnutrition rose and Havana became known for its brothels, casinos, and US gangsters.

In this context, rebellion was inevitable. A small group of guerrillas led by Fidel Castro was able to mobilize the Cuban people from their base in the Sierra Maestra and wreak havoc on the government during the Revolution of 1956–8. On 1 January 1959 Batista fled the country and Fidel Castro took power.

Castro introduced a number of policies which improved the lives of the average Cuban, including free education, free health care, housing for all, land reform, and wage rises. Life expectancy rose, infant mortality fell, many infectious diseases were eradicated, and Cubans are among the healthiest and best educated people in the world. However, US antagonism pushed Castro into the arms of the Soviet Union and, under communism, Cubans found themselves deprived of many liberties such as travel, freedom of speech, and press freedom, as well as democracy and other human rights. The fall of the Soviet Union and the loss of economic support revealed structural problems which have been difficult to solve.

Fidel handed the reins of power to his brother Raúl in 2006 and died in 2016. Raúl sought a rapprochement with the US, culminating in the visit of President Barack Obama and his family in 2016, but the trade embargo remains in place pending further reforms by the Cuban government.

CLIMATE

Cuba enjoys a subtropical climate with plenty of sunshine and warm weather tempered by northeast trade winds, but it can be hot and humid. The east is hotter than the west and carnival in Santiago de Cuba in July can be a cauldron. The driest time of year is December to April and this is considered high tourist season. June is the beginning of hurricane season, which goes on until November. Heavy rains can fall at any time, but most of the serious storms have occurred in September–November. In winter there can be some cold days and nights if a cold front comes down the eastern seaboard of the US.

Lighting up in Havana

Trinidad street life

POPULATION

Cuba has a population of 11.3 million, of whom 2.1 million live in the city of Havana, making it the largest metropolitan area in the Caribbean. Access to birth control has considerably reduced the birth rate and illegal migration to the US by frustrated young Cubans has kept the population relatively stable since 2000.

Cubans are multi-ethnic and there is some blurring of the lines over whether people call themselves black or white. Most white immigrants have come from Spain, although other European countries are also represented, while most black immigrants were slaves brought from West Africa. After the abolition of slavery, there was also a wave of Chinese immigration. There are very few Cubans

---

DON'T LEAVE CUBA WITHOUT

Visiting the Fábrica de Arte Cubano in Vedado, Havana. A contemporary cultural experience to beat all others, with art, fashion, music, food and drink all under one roof in an old industrial building – *the* place to be in Havana. See page 115.

Strolling around the orchidarium in Soroa. Any lover of orchids will be enchanted by the 700 varieties grown here, most of which flower from December to March. See page 43.

Visiting the Che Monument and Mausoleum in Santa Clara. If you've had a poster of Che Guevara on your wall as a student, or seen the movies of his life, you will want to see Cuba's homage to the guerrilla and the eternal flame which burns for him and his comrades. See page 71.

Enjoying a sunset cocktail at La Escalinata, Trinidad. Live bands play at this open air bar on the steps beside the church as you sip a refreshing mojito and watch the honeyed hues of the setting sun reflecting on pastel colonial buildings. See page 62.

Birdwatching in the Zapata peninsula. A Unesco Biosphere Reserve, home to 190 species of bird, is a fascinating experience for any bird lover. See page 52.

Hiking to La Comandancia de la Plata. Imagine you're a revolutionary and do the hike in the Sierra Maestra to Fidel's command post. See page 85.

Finding an isolated beach and doing nothing. Playa Paraíso on Cayo Santa María is indeed a paradise, away from the hotel strip, a huge expanse of white sand lapped by shallow water of many turquoise hues. See page 76.

Dancing the night away. Santiago de Cuba is known for its music and nightlife with no shortage of venues for traditional *son*, *trova* or *boleros*, but this is the place to get up and salsa. See page 116.

Staying in a *casa particular*. The best way of getting to know Cubans is to rent a room in a family home. Your hosts will be happy to chat about the vagaries of life on the island and serve you the freshest local food. Lobster anyone? See page 100.

who can trace their ancestry to the Taíno Amerindians, but their influence lives on in local vocabulary and place names as well as some facial features.

LOCAL CUSTOMS

Museums are usually (but not always) closed on Monday and Sunday afternoon. Tourist sights do not close for lunch. Although Cubans generally eat their main meal at lunchtime, tourists are expected to eat in the evening. Cuba is hot and many women wear skimpy tops, but bathing suits are for the beach and should not be worn around town. Dress decently to go into a church or temple. You may be asked to cover your shoulders if they are bare. There are often dress codes at nightclubs: Cubans dress smartly to go out at night and men are expected to wear long trousers and shirts. In Havana, particularly, nightlife doesn't get going until midnight and many places stay open until dawn at weekends.

POLITICS AND ECONOMICS

Cuba remains an outpost of Communism despite the death of Fidel Castro in 2016 and is a one-party state. Raúl Castro was formerly head of the Armed Forces and the military wields significant power, both in politics and economics. The military, or its enterprises, owns most of the coastal land being developed for tourism and makes money from joint ventures with foreign investors.

Private enterprise is limited, taxed, and strictly controlled. Cubans are allowed to rent rooms to foreigners and to run restaurants, as well as other businesses in tourism such as taxis and tour guides. This allows them to earn hard currency and has lifted them out of poverty, but a split has opened up between those who earn foreign exchange and those who don't. The average wage for someone who works for the state is the equivalent of only US$25 a month, often supplemented by stealing from the employer and selling goods on the black market. Raúl

Sunbathing in Trinidad

Havana skyline at sunset

Castro aims to unify the two currencies, the *peso Cubano* and the *peso convertible* to eliminate distortions, but a timescale has not been announced.

TOP TIPS FOR VISITING CUBA

Book car hire in advance. There is a shortage of rental cars on the island and, if you want to get to places off the beaten track, car hire or taxis are the only means of transport. Demand is particularly high in July–August when Cubans are on holiday, but the high tourist season of December–April is also busy. All companies are state-owned and there are frequent complaints about inefficiency and lack of maintenance as well as expense. Breakdowns and punctures are common on dirt roads so for peace of mind choose Rex, the most expensive company but with the best cars and good, English-speaking, customer service. Only non-US credit cards are accepted. The alternative is to pay cash in advance.

Protect your skin. Many people underestimate the power of the Caribbean sun and cooling sea breezes mask its strength. Use a high factor sunscreen on all exposed skin, wear loose-fitting clothing, a hat, and sunglasses. Take extra precautions with children and limit the time spent in the sun.

Book accommodations early. In high season you are advised to book hotels and *casas particulares* well in advance. Tourist hot spots such as Trinidad and Viñales are often full and visitors have been forced to sleep on the beach or in the plaza for lack of a reservation. Casas *particulares* should always be reconfirmed the day before arrival or you may lose your reservation to passing trade.

Do not underestimate distances and travel times. It takes around six hours to get from Havana to Trinidad and four hours to either Viñales or Santa Clara, so day trips are not recommended unless you are prepared for a long day's travel. It is always more comfortable to stay for a night or two and experience the nightlife in each town.

Take care with the dual exchange rate. Do not change more than US$10 into *pesos Cubanos* and then only if you are going to more remote places. Tourists have to pay in *pesos convertibles* for all accommodations, restaurants, and transportation and opportunities for using *pesos Cubanos* are rare.

Master the art of queuing. Cubans are used to standing in line for many of their daily needs and have perfected a system allowing them to wander off without losing their place. You might not even notice there is a line. Always ask who is the last in line – *el último* – and then tell the next person that you are the last. Failure to observe this courtesy when queuing for currency exchange or bus tickets can result in angry exchanges.

Book internal flights in advance. You can travel by bus or car the length of the island from Havana to Santiago de Cuba or Baracoa and return by plane, but it is best to book your flight from abroad because of high demand, particularly in December–May and July–August.

Lobster, simply prepared

FOOD AND DRINK

Cuban food is simple and seasonal with Spanish and African influences and relying heavily on rice and beans, but some of the world's best rum cocktails originated here.

During the 'Special Period', the tough years after the collapse of the Soviet Union when there were shortages of absolutely everything, Cuba became the land of 'no hay', which means 'there isn't any'. People had to learn to cook with whatever was available. Lean times forced Cubans to improvise, stretching and enhancing rice with whatever was available, planning vegetarian meals in a culinary culture obsessed with meat.

Since then, the opening of farmers' markets (*agropecuarios*) has made a wider choice of ingredients available. These are markets where farmers sell their surplus produce, after the state has bought its quota, and you will find a wide range of goods on sale, from fresh fruit and vegetables to meat, eggs, and honey. Much of this produce is grown in *organopónicos*, organic urban allotments on any available space, originally started in Havana to provide the capital with fresh vegetables and avoid transportation costs.

Cuba still has rationing, but the ration card no longer provides enough to live on. Bread, rice, beans, and coffee are rationed in limited quantities but families have to buy the balance of their needs at market prices. Cuba is not self-sufficient in food and most staples are imported. Shops sell imported tins of food, crackers, biscuits, cookies, which are useful snacks for a long journey, all priced in *pesos convertibles* (CUC$).

LOCAL CUISINE

Cuban staples

If Cuban creole (*criollo*) cuisine had a national dish, it would, without question, be roast pork (*puerco* or *cerdo*) served with black beans (*frijoles*), white rice (*arroz*), and plantains (*plátanos*), which is what people eat at New Year celebrations. Rice and beans are traditionally prepared in two forms: kidney beans with rice, known as *moros y cristianos* (Moors and Christians), or black beans with rice (*congrí*). A delicious soupy stew of black beans (*potaje*) is sometimes served alongside plain white rice. Root vegetables are also popular accompaniments, particularly *yuca* (also called *cassava*, a starchy tuber), *malanga*, and *boniato*. Malanga is not unlike *yuca*, and *boniato* is a tasty kind of sweet potato.

Chicken (*pollo*) appears on many menus – invariably fried. Fish (*pescado*)

Black beans, a criollo staple

Pineapples for sale, Viñales

is usually *pargo* (snapper) or any plain steak of white fish that is simply called *pescado*. Lobster (*langosta*) is generally the most expensive item on the menu but widely available for tourists.

The ingredients, herbs, and spices most used in traditional Cuban cooking are cumin, oregano, parsley, sour oranges, and *ajo* – garlic. *Sofrito*, a paste of chopped onion, garlic, and green pepper sizzled in oil, is the basis of many dishes. In these days of scarce ingredients, a popular seasoning for vegetables and meat is a tasty mixture of sour orange, garlic, and oil, called *mojo*.

Fruit and desserts

Fruit in Cuba is a delight, and so are the juices made from it. Everything is harvested in season, when it is at its peak: sweet, juicy pineapples, grapefruits that need no sugar, mangos like you've never tasted before, and bananas – the small, chunky ones are the best. Avocados, too, are at their perfect, creamy best when picked straight from the tree. Unless you buy it in markets you are most likely to come across fruit on the breakfast table of a *casa particular* or the breakfast buffet in a hotel. Despite being plentiful and cheap it is rarely offered as a dessert. Freshly squeezed fruit juices can be found in many bars, in whatever variety is most available – ask for *jugo natural* to get the real thing.

The role of dessert on Cuban menus is usually played by ice cream (and it is

generally very good, too) or the ubiquitous *flan*, a caramel custard. Cubans do, on the whole, have a sweet tooth – you just need to look in a bakery window at the fluffy pink and baby-blue iced confections to realize that. If you are in Cuba for Mother's Day (the second Sunday in May) you will see special versions of these cakes being handed out of bakers' storefronts to waiting crowds and, everywhere you go, notice people carrying them home, often one in each hand, or balancing them on bicycle handlebars.

In the east of the island, try the *cucuruchu* for the ultimate in sweetness. This is grated coconut, sometimes

The versatile plantain

Cuban cooking exalts lowly ingredients. Take, for instance, the plantain, *el plátano*. You can fry it ripe (*maduro*) in slices, or green (*verde*) in paper-thin chips (*chicharitas*). You can fry thicker wedges of green plantain, squash them, and fry them again for *tostones*. You can boil plantain chunks, ripe or green, mash them with a fork, drizzle with olive oil, and sprinkle with crunchy fried pork rinds for *fu fú* – a dish of West African origin and something of an acquired taste. You can fill mashed plantains with *picadillo*, minced meat, and melted white cheese to make a *pastel de plátano*. In fact, you can do just about anything except eat them uncooked.

Waiting for customers in Havana

flavored with fruit juice and (mostly) sugar and sold in ingeniously fashioned banana-leaf wrappings.

WHERE TO EAT

Eating out

State-owned restaurants can be identified by the credit card stickers on the door. A few are good, particularly in Havana, but most are boring, offering poor quality food and even worse service. They charge in CUC$. They do, however, offer some variety in cuisine, with Italian, Spanish, or Chinese the most common. Resort hotels usually have buffet and à la carte restaurants where you can find something you like, although the food often appears recycled or reheated. At the cheaper end of the state sector are fast-food joints, burger bars, or fried chicken places for a greasy snack. Bars and cafés have snacks and light meals for lunch but sandwiches are usually cheese, ham, or cheese and ham, with stodgy white bread.

Street stalls charge in *pesos Cubanos*, selling lunch-time sandwiches and stodgy pizza, but check these carefully if you are concerned about hygiene. Most are best avoided.

For many years after the 1959 revolution, family-run restaurants were illegal, as was virtually every kind of private enterprise. They operated clandestinely, yet everyone knew where they were; even policemen and party members could be seen eating in them. Then, in 1994, the law was changed and these establishments, called *paladares*, could start doing business more openly. Cuba was suddenly full of *paladares* offering cheap home cooking – usually serving the traditional menu of pork, beans, and rice.

Paladares are obliged to register with the state, meet strict public-health standards, and pay both a license fee and taxes. The state has relaxed some of the initial restrictions, particularly on the number of covers and employing staff from outside the family. As a result, there has been another explosion in the number of privately-run restaurants, many of which have invested money sent by family in Miami in equipment and décor and are very good.

Eating in

The alternative to eating out is to eat in your *casa particular*. This may lack the atmosphere or cuisine of a good *paladar*, but has the advantage of allowing you to order exactly what you want, when you want it. You can be sure that the food will be bought and cooked fresh that day and any special dietary requirements can be catered for. Vegetarians often find that this is by far the best option, and many *casa* owners have become quite skilled at providing meat-free meals. You may need to check, however, that beans are not cooked with the traditional lard, and some vegetarians prefer to travel with

The best rum on the island

their own cooking oil, which they lend to their hosts.

DRINKS

Cuban rum

The first thing that comes to mind when one thinks of drinking in Cuba is rum. Along with cigars, this is Cuba's best-known product. Rum, of course, is a sugar-based alcohol, and Cuba has always had plenty of sugar. The best-known and biggest brand is Havana Club. There are various types, but you will most often find Añejo 3 Años, Añejo Reserva, and Añejo 7 Años, of which the latter is the best. There is also a white rum, Añejo Blanco.

A good, aged rum (*ron* in Spanish) can be drunk neat, like a brandy or whisky (ask for *ron de siete años*), but white or three-year-old rum is used as the basis of Cuba's famous cocktails: the mojito (rum, lime, mint, and soda water), the daiquirí (rum, lime juice, sugar, and crushed ice), the piña colada (rum with pineapple juice and coconut), and the Cuba Libre. The latter – which means Free Cuba – originated at the end of the 1898 War of Independence and was made with rum and Coca-Cola.

Beer and wine

As well as rum, Cubans are also very fond of beer, which is hardly surprising in this hot climate. Cristal, a light beer made by the Mayabe Brewery, can be found all over the island. The same brewery makes Mayabe, ordinary and extra, which has more flavor. Hatuey beer is made in Havana but is not always easy to find. Bucanero is made in Holguín and found mostly in the east, while Tínimo, made in Camagüey, can be difficult to obtain outside that city.

You can buy wine in hotels and restaurants, but don't expect to find it everywhere. There is small-scale wine production in the west, sold under the Soroa label, but most of the available wine comes from Chile or Argentina.

Home-grown coffee

Cuba produces and consumes some excellent coffee, mainly Arabica, the majority of which is grown in the Sierra Maestra region where the mountainous climate is ideal. Ask for a *café con leche* if you want coffee with hot milk – this is normally drunk at breakfast time. A *café cubano* or *cafecito* (little coffee) is small and strong like an espresso, except that it will come ready sweetened unless you ask for it 'sin azúcar'.

Food and drink prices

Prices are for a two-course meal, not including drinks.
$ = less than $10
$$ = $10–20
$$$ = $20–40
$$$$ = $40 and up

Bolívar cigars

SHOPPING

Nobody goes to Cuba for the shopping. One of the most striking things is the lack of consumer goods – along with the lack of advertising. However, two of the things that Cuba is most famous for – cigars and rum – are easy to find and make the best gifts.

The shopping scene in Havana has been upgraded as the old buildings have been renovated. The main commercial streets of the pre-revolutionary era are now gradually coming to life, with new and more up-market stores opening all the time. Habana Vieja tends to have smart, expensive stores, geared specifically at tourists, in the renovated streets, but few tourists go to Cuba to buy Italian designer labels.

CIGARS AND RUM

Both cigars and rum can be purchased in the big hotels or tourist stores, or directly from the cigar factories and rum distilleries that offer tours. Cigars can be bought on any visit to a factory, or specialist shop called a Casa del Habano. Hotel cigar stores all have large humidors and usually well-informed staff. If you have left it until the last minute, you can buy cigars at the airport, but the selection is smaller. Don't be tempted to buy cigars from hustlers on the street: most of them are fakes made from cheap tobacco or even banana leaves, whatever the labels say.

Rum can be bought just about everywhere. Habana Club is the best: the cheapest variety is the three-year-old white rum; the most expensive (and this only means about CUC$12) is the *añejo siete años*; in between come the *añejo cinco años* and the *añejo reserva* – these three are all dark rums of different ages. Limited edition specialty rums are also available at much higher prices, which you are unlikely to find abroad.

COFFEE AND CACAO

Cuban coffee is well worth purchasing, too; Cubita is the best brand. However, when traveling around, you may come across families who grow and roast their own beans. This makes the best souvenir if they will sell it to you.

Cacao is grown in the east and chocolate is made in Baracoa. It can be rather grainy. More refined chocolate is made in Havana but is not yet up to the standard of other Caribbean producers.

MUSIC AND CRAFTS

If you fall under the spell of Cuban music, as most people do, you will want to splash out on a few CDs. Many hotels have a reasonable selection, but keep an eye open for Artex stores, which have a

Havana souvenirs

Colorful paintings in Santiago

better-than-average choice. Many of the groups that serenade you in Old Havana and elsewhere have their own CDs for sale. The recording quality is not the best, and the music may not sound quite as good once you get it home, but they can make good, nostalgic mementoes.

The legalization of private enterprise has meant that many Cubans have started painting pictures and making jewelry, embroidery, ceramics, leather goods, and musical instruments. One of the best places for crafts in Cuba is the Feria de Artesanía, in Almacenes San José, on San Pedro (Avenida del Puerto), just beyond the ferry for Regla. You will find jewelry, leather goods, carved wooden items, and more. You are expected to haggle.

Foreign interest in Santería and other Afro-Cuban religions has also spawned the proliferation of souvenirs related to these cults, from the colorful necklaces associated with Santería to sculpted figures of the gods (*orishas*).

The band's CD for sale in Trinidad

BOOKS AND ART

Second-hand books and fascinating newspapers and magazines from the pre- and early revolutionary era are worth looking out for, too. Across Cuba you will find people selling books in the street or from the front of their houses. The biggest collection is to be found in the stalls in the Plaza de Armas in Old Havana.

Many book stores are depressingly empty of new titles, but books of obvious interest to tourists are being published for sale in CUC stores. The range of titles is improving, but stock is often dominated by illustrated books about Cuba, expensive reprints of Cuban revolutionary volumes (the speeches of Che Guevara or the works of José Martí, etc.), and a limited number of novels in Spanish by "safe" authors (García Márquez is a favorite).

Visitors who wish to buy Cuban art should note that they need an export permit. State-run stores and galleries will issue this automatically. You also need a permit if you buy a work from a street market or artist – no matter how inexpensive. Sometimes, the artist will issue a permit, but otherwise you must go to the Registro Nacional de Bienes Culturales. It is important to get one, otherwise your purchases will be confiscated at the airport. This is also true for antiques and antiquarian books, over 50 years old. For details of customs regulations for taking cigars and rum out of the country, see www.aduana.co.cu.

Tropicana dancer

ENTERTAINMENT

Cuba pulsates with music, rhythm and dance, ranging from trios that play traditional son, guarachas and boleros to Afro–Cuban folkloric groups, jazz, ballet, and full-scale cabaret while young Cubans listen to rock, rap, and reggaeton.

Music and Cuba are synonymous and in no other communist country have music and revolution marched so closely, hand in hand. Cuba has produced a staggering number of world class artists, dancers, musicians, and movie makers. Many have left the country to seek their fortunes elsewhere, but you are still guaranteed an artistic and cultural feast when visiting.

Visitors are never far from music, with scorching jazz drumming rising from basement bars and sweet guitar melodies in Buena Vista style, drifting from pavement cafés. The song *Guantanamera* is as ubiquitous as images of Che Guevara and the evocative *Chan Chan* is a reminder of the impact the *Buena Vista Social Club* movie and album has had on the surge of tourism since the late 1990s.

Many tourists visit Cuba for the salsa dancing, often on special packages, and leading salsa bands like Los Van Van can often be seen performing live.

BARS AND NIGHTCLUBS

Havana is the epicenter of nightlife and clubs start late, around midnight. However, some places offer early shows, even matinées, for the younger crowd, which can be useful if you are traveling with teenagers. The emphasis is always on dancing, whether it is salsa, R&B, rock, or any other style.

One very popular venue is the Café Cantante, underneath the Teatro Nacional in the Plaza de la Revolución. Starting at 10pm, live bands play on until dawn at weekends. There are also very popular matinées here. The Teatro Bertolt Brecht also has a basement café/bar open nightly, but to hear contemporary fusion bands playing live, visit Tuesday, Thursday or Friday nights for 'No se lo digas a nadie' (Don't tell anyone). The most popular night spot for the in-crowd in Havana is currently the Fábrica de Arte Cubano in Vedado, a fusion of art gallery, bar, restaurant, and music venue, but expect lines outside for some events.

CABARET

Internationally famous as one of the best cabaret shows in the world, the Tropicana, opened in 1931 (Calle 72 4504, entre Ave 43 y 45, Marianao), has all the glitz and glamour of a casino show, but now without the gambling. Shows are

At the Casa de la Trova in Santiago de Cuba

nightly except Monday, weather permitting, as it is an outdoor amphitheater and cancellations are common in the rainy season. There are also cabaret shows in a few hotels: Copa Room at the Riviera, Parisien at the Hotel Nacional and the Salón Rojo at the Caprí, left over from the gangster era, as well as a more Caribbean version at the Club Tropicana Santiago in the east.

JAZZ

Jazz is central to Cuban music, though many exponents are easier to catch live during foreign tours. Irakere, the 15-piece group founded in 1970 by pianist Chucho Valdés, fused North American jazz idioms and has operated as a university for young soloists.

In Vedado, Havana, head for the Jazz Café, Galerías del Paseo esq 1, which puts on two live performances, at 9.30 pm and 11pm, with top performers, including Chucho Valdés, being welcomed by a knowledgeable and enthusiastic crowd. A more intimate, basement bar is La Zorra y El Cuervo (The Fox and the Crow), Ave 23 y O, where jazz musicians squeeze in with the audience for performances from 11pm. Get there earlier if you want a table.

CASA DE LA TROVA

Every town in Cuba has a Casa de la Trova, where live traditional music can be heard and danced to. *Trova's* guitar melodies, vocal harmonies, sensual rhythms, and lyrics inspired by the country life and work, patriotic or revolutionary themes, originates from troubadours' peripatetic life playing songs alongside soldiers during the War of Independence in the 19th century and the Revolution in the 1950s. The latter spawned a *nueva trova* movement linked to Latin America's 1960s revolutions and key figures Pablo Milanés and Silvio Rodríguez are now superstar elder statesmen who perform internationally.

Festivals

Cuba offers a large number of cultural festivals worth taking into account when planning a visit. Carnival is not pre-Lent and the best is in Santiago de Cuba in July, a hot and steamy music and dance extravaganza which goes on for a week. An International Jazz festival in April attracts international performers (Herbie Hancock, Chucho Valdes) and audiences. The International Festival of the New Latin American Cinema in December is the most important film festival in Latina America when the best movies and documentaries are shown in Havana cinemas. The International Ballet Festival of Havana, held every other year in October/November, attracts dancers and choreographers from around the world with stunning performances of new works and workshops in theaters around the country.

Sea wonders, María la Gorda

OUTDOOR ACTIVITIES

Any number of activities are available to tempt you off your sun bed. Cuba is sports mad and athleticism is prized but you don't need to be super fit to enjoy the great outdoors.

Beach resorts offer watersports such as diving, snorkeling, and fishing, while on land you can be active hiking, running, cycling, horse-riding, or bird-watching. The most popular spectator sports include basketball, boxing, and the all-important baseball, the national sport which provokes lively debate.

SCUBA DIVING

Cuba is almost surrounded by reefs, which are in good condition and teeming with assorted marine creatures. State-owned dive shops at the beach resort areas offer a variety of diving, from reefs, walls, and caves to wrecks and shark feeding. There are some private dive instructors, but they are only allowed to offer shore dives; boats are government property. Some of the best diving is in very remote areas, such as Isla de la Juventud and María la Gorda, but diving and snorkeling are rewarding in the Bay of Pigs, much easier to get to, where you can do both in cenotes, limestone sinkholes and caverns full of colorful fish, as well as in the sea.

FISHING

Ernest Hemingway was a keen fisherman and wrote about the delights of the Cuban cays in his novels while Fidel Castro also loved a day's deep-sea fishing. There are several marinas around the island offering boats to catch marlin, swordfish, wahoo, and other game fish and there are often tournaments. Bonefishing is also excellent in the flats of the Zapata peninsula while fly fishing is also good off Cayo Largo or the Jardines de la Reina archipelago off the south coast. There is also freshwater fishing, which takes place in lakes and reservoirs, where the main catch is large-mouth bass, known locally as *trucha*, or trout.

HIKING

There is good hiking in any of the mountain ranges where there are forests, waterfalls, and pools for cooling off amongst the lush vegetation. Guides are compulsory in the National Parks and there are plenty of organized walks and excursions for all abilities. Some of the best hiking is in the

Cycling in Camagüey   *Baseball is a national obsession*

Sierra Maestra, where you can sign up for multi-day hiking up Pico Turquino, the highest peak on the island. The Parque Nacional Humboldt near Baracoa is exceptionally rewarding for nature enthusiasts. The December–April dry season is best for hiking but you should expect rain and mud at any time of year in the rainforest.

CYCLING

Cuba is very bike-friendly, in that it is the main form of transport for many people. Bicycles and bicitaxis clog the roads in many towns and all transportation moves at their pace. Outside towns you should watch out for potholes, while gravel roads can play havoc with your tyres, but at least most of Cuba is relatively flat.

Some hotels rent basic bicycles to tourists to explore their surroundings, but keen cyclists should book a package deal or join a charity group, which will enable you to travel long distances with someone else taking care of your luggage and accommodations. Really serious cyclists take their own bikes with them and all the equipment and spares they could possibly need. If you are traveling independently, it is worth trying to book *casas particulares* with ground floor rooms so you don't have to carry your bike and gear up several flights of stairs at the end of a long, hot day. Competitive cyclists can enter a number of international competitions held in Cuba, of which the longest is the Vuelta a Cuba, a staged road race running the length of the island.

BASEBALL

Cubans are baseball mad and follow their local teams with a religious fervor. Fans gather in *plazas* to discuss recent matches, many of which are shown on television for those who can't get to the stadium. Children who show promise are send to sports academies for intensive training and development and then progress to their provincial teams. All players are amateurs, but elite players are subsidized and given special rewards. Unfortunately this has not prevented defections whenever the national side has played abroad, and the standard and success of the Cuban team has consequently declined.

There are 16 provincial baseball teams divided geographically into east and west. The Cuba National League has a national provincial championship, the Serie Nacional, a super-provincial series, the Súper Liga, which aids in the selection of the Cuban national baseball team, and seven other leagues. The season runs from November to April and this is followed by play-offs culminating in the National Championship. In Havana, the best place to see a baseball match is at the Estadio Latinoamericano, south of the center in the district of Cerro and home to the Industriales team, also known as Los Azules.

Havana harbor circa 1639

HISTORY: KEY DATES

Ever since the arrival of Spanish conquistadores, the political history of Cuba has been one of resistance and struggle against autocracy and repression.

EARLY HISTORY

c. 3500–4000BC	First human settlement of pre-ceramic hunter-gatherer people.
AD600–1000	Arrival of agricultural Taíno peoples from Orinoco basin.

THE SPANISH COLONY

1492	Columbus lands on Cuban soil.
1511	Diego Velázquez's expedition begins European settlement.
1517	First shipment of slaves from Africa to work on the plantations.
1555	Fortresses are built to protect Havana and Santiago from pirates.
1717	Tobacco trade declared a monopoly of Spanish Crown.
1762–3	British expedition occupies Havana, then swaps Cuba for Florida.
1789	Slave trade thrives as sugar becomes most valuable export.
1868–78	First War of Independence against Spain.
1886	Abolition of slavery in Cuba.
1895–8	Second War of Independence.
1895	José Martí, poet-founder of the Cuban Revolutionary Party, killed.

DICTATORSHIP AND REVOLUTION

1898	US defeats Spanish. Cubans excluded from peace process.
1901	Platt Amendment allows the US to intervene in Cuban affairs.
1902	Tomás Estrada Palma becomes first president of Cuban Republic.
1903	Lease of Guantánamo begins.
1906–9	Marines invade to protect US interests.
1912	Afro-Cuban Black Uprising savagely repressed.
1925–33	Gerardo Machado in power. General strike forces him to flee.
1934	Fulgencio Batista holds power as president. Abrogation of Platt Amendment but Guantánamo left in US control.

Raúl and Fidel Castro at a military parade in 1996

1940–4	Batista serves term as elected president.
1952	Batista seizes power in coup.
1953	Failed attack on Moncada garrison, led by Fidel Castro.
1956	Castro's revolutionaries begin rebel war in the Sierra Maestra.
1959	Batista flees. Castro becomes prime minister.

COMMUNISM

1960	Trade treaty signed with Soviet Union. Foreign-owned companies and banks nationalized.
1961	US breaks off diplomatic relations. Castro proclaims Socialist nature of Revolution. US-sponsored Bay of Pigs invasion fails.
1962	President Kennedy imposes embargo. Cuban Missile Crisis brings world to brink of nuclear war.
1980	120,000 refugees leave for Miami during Mariel boatlift.
1991	Russian aid to Cuba axed after fall of the Soviet Union. Food and fuel shortages.
1993–4	Worst economic hardship of the Special Period. Dollar legalized.
1994	40,000 refugees flee Cuba for the US; the US ends its open-door policy for Cuban immigrants.
1996	US embargo tightens.

21ST CENTURY

2002	Nearly half the sugar mills close; 100,000 workers lose jobs.
2003	Crackdown on political dissidents brings worldwide criticism.
2006	Fidel undergoes surgery. Replaced temporarily by brother Raúl.
2008	Raúl Castro officially becomes president. Hurricanes hit Cuba.
2009	Raúl imposes sweeping cabinet changes and austerity measures.
2012	Hurricane Sandy hits the east, causing death and destruction.
2013	Cubans allowed to travel abroad.
2014	Presidents Castro and Obama trigger thaw of Cuban–US relations.
2015	US tourists visit Cuba on approved programs. Charter flights begin.
2016	US President Obama visits Cuba. Fidel Castro dies.
2017	Repeal of 'wet foot, dry foot' policy leaves thousands of Cubans stranded abroad trying to enter the US. Trump presidency halts progress in improving relations. Hurricanes Irma and José batter Cuba, leaving a trail of devastation and 10 people dead.

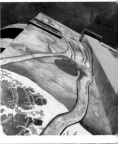

BEST ROUTES

Cruising along the Malecón

OLD HAVANA SIGHTS

Palaces, mansions, fortresses, and churches jostle for your attention, with architectural delights round every corner. This fine Spanish colonial city should be toured on foot, but always look up to witness the balcony life of its residents.

DISTANCE: 3 miles (4.8 km) of walking
TIME: A full day
START: Castillo de la Punta
END: Almacenes San José
POINTS TO NOTE: Avoid Monday if you want to visit museums as most of them close that day. Make sure to wear shoes you are comfortable walking in and carry a bottle of water to avoid dehydration.

Renovation of Old Havana is a huge task, but many of the grandest buildings have now been restored, to be used as museums, galleries, shops, restaurants, or boutique hotels. The grandest and largest hotels have generally kept only the colonial façade, but all are in keeping with the rest of the city. There are no skyscrapers and several of the streets are pedestrianized, for a relaxing experience.

Old Havana is not a living museum, however, and much of the residential area to the south remains in a poor state, to be repaired when funds permit.

As an alternative to the state hotels, many residents own casas particulares (private rooms) if you want to immerse yourself in the life of the colonial city and spend a few days exploring further.

THE PRADO

From the 16th-century **Castillo de San Salvador de la Punta ❶** you can see the old city in its geographical and strategic context. Situated at the mouth of the entrance to Havana's harbor, the fort guarded shipping together with the larger fortresses across the water, El Morro and La Cabaña. A chain was raised at night across the channel to prevent pirates gaining entry to the Spanish merchant fleets. The view is spectacular as you look along the Malecón, the seafront drive stretching all the way round the coast, and it is a great place for people watching or spotting old US automobiles.

Head inland, southwest, down the magnificent **Paseo de Martí**, known as the **Prado ❷**. This tree-lined promenade dividing Centro from Old Havana was once a walkway outside the

Parque Central art

The Capitolio

city walls, but by the time it was completed in 1852, the walls had collapsed. Traffic runs either side of the marble and stone pedestrian avenue, which is used as a public open space: schoolchildren having sports lessons or playtime, impromptu concerts or art markets are all found here. Overlooking the Prado is the **Hotel Mercure Sevilla**, once a notorious mafia hangout and the setting for Graham Greene's *Our Man in Havana*, where his secret agent stayed in room 501. The end of the Prado opens out on to the elegant Parque Central.

PARQUE CENTRAL

The **Parque Central** ❸, with its stately royal palms and white marble statue of José Martí, is always a hive of activity. It is surrounded by elegant buildings, each one of them with a history to tell. The **Hotel Inglaterra**, which dates from 1875, was popular with early travelers from England and its streetside bar and café still attract tourists who come here for people watching and listening to live music – although be warned you may be hassled. Next door, the newly restored, baroque **Gran Teatro de la Habana Alicia Alonso** dates from 1837 and is a beautifully ornate building. Ballet is its specialty (although you can also find opera and other theater performances) and you can sometimes sneak a peek at a rehearsal if you can't get tickets.

On the southwest corner of the Parque Central, the **Capitolio** ❹ occupies a whole block. Built in 1929–32 by General Machado as the new presidential and governmental palace, it closely resembles the Capitol in Washington DC and was designed to flatter the US. It was still being restored in 2017 and when completed will be the home of the National Assembly. Outside the Capitolio there are always a number of 1950s limousines – Buicks, Chevrolets, Packards, Chryslers – but unlike the many beat-up models you see around town, these have shiny bodywork and gleaming hubcaps: they are taxis waiting to take tourists on a tour around the city.

Half of the east side of the Parque Central is taken up by the **Arte Universal** section of the Fine Arts Museum: the **Museo Nacional Palacio de Bellas Artes** ❺ (www.museonacional.cult.cu; Tue–Sat 9am–5pm, Sun 10am–2pm; charge, combined ticket for this and the Arte Cubano section, see below). The museum contains Latin America's largest collection of antiquities, as well as works by Goya, Rubens, Velázquez, Turner, Gainsborough, and Canaletto, many of which were left behind by Batista's family and cronies when they fled after the Revolution.

Next to the museum is **El Floridita** (Obispo esq Monserrate; 11.30am–midnight), a favorite haunt of Hemingway as well as of the Hollywood set who came to Havana in the 1950s –

The Art Deco Edificio Bacardí

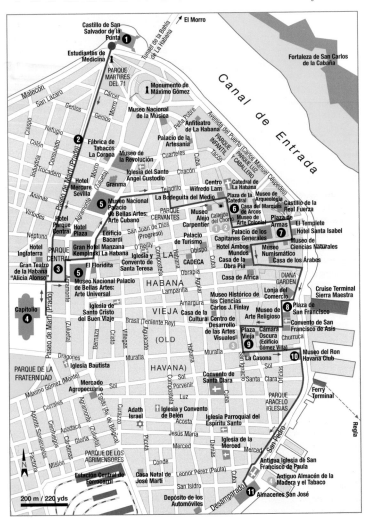

The Cathedral seen from the Palacio de los Condes de Casa Bayona

Errol Flynn, Frank Sinatra, Ava Gardner, Gary Cooper, and Marlene Dietrich were all regulars. Pop in to try one of Hemingway's daiquirís, although the bar and restaurant are now plush and expensive, far from the informal place he knew. From here walk northeast along Avenida de los Misiones, past the beautiful Art Deco **Edificio Bacardí**, topped with the statue of a giant bat, which was the family emblem. Dating from 1929, it is a strange mixture of Swedish granite, Cuban limestone, tiles, and terracotta, resembling a giant three-dimensional mosaic.

The best museum in the city is the **Arte Cubano** section of the Fine Arts Museum (see times above), which contains the largest collection of works by Cuban artists in the country. The excellent 20th-century section includes pieces by Wifredo Lam, Carlos Enríquez, René Portocarrero, and Eduard Abela. Start on the third floor with the colonial art and work your way down to the present day. On the ground floor are temporary exhibitions and a shop.

PLAZA DE LA CATEDRAL

Head east now to the oldest part of the city, walking along Tejadillo, three blocks, turn right down Habana for a block, then left along Empedrado. You will pass another of Hemingway's drinking haunts, **La Bodeguita del Medio**, once popular as a meeting place for authors such as Alejo Car-

pentier (whose house is also on this street), Nicolás Guillén, and others, as it was next to a print shop. Now it is famous for having perfected the mojito, for the graffiti on the walls and for being on the tourist trail.

Further along, on the corner, is the **Centro Wifredo Lam** (San Ignacio esq Empedrados; Mon–Sat 10am–5pm), a cultural center dedicated to one of Cuba's most famous 20th-century artists (1902–82). It exhibits the works of contemporary artists from Cuba and the rest of the world and is one of the venues for the Havana Arts Biennial.

The beautiful **Plaza de la Catedral** ❻ is dominated by the baroque cathedral: **Catedral de la Virgen María de la Concepción Inmaculada** (Mon–Fri 9am–5pm, Sat, Sun 9am–noon; charge to go up the tower), but better known as the San Cristóbal Cathedral after the city's patron saint. The Jesuits started the construction, but they were expelled in 1767. Completed in 1777, it became a cathedral in 1793. Note the asymmetrical bell towers. Inside, the altar is of Carrara marble inlaid with gold, silver, and onyx.

Around the plaza are some lovely old mansions. The **Casa de Lombillo** was built in 1741 by a wealthy slave trader. Beside it is the **Casa del Marqués de Arcos**, built in 1742 for the royal treasurer. The **Palacio de los Condes de Casa Bayona**, opposite the Cathedral, was built in 1720 for the governor and has a lovely central courtyard,

Castillo de la Real Fuerza

some stunning stained glass and superb wooden ceilings. It now houses the **Museo de Arte Colonial** (Tue–Sun 9.30am–5pm; charge).

On the southwest corner of the square is the **Callejón de Chorro**, a tiny cul-de-sac where an Art Nouveau building houses the Experimental Workshop of Graphic Arts. You can watch artists at work and items are for sale. If you are in need of lunch, **Bianchini** (see ❶) offers handmade sweet and savory baked goods, freshly ground coffee, and organic chocolate. Alternatively, **Esto No Es Un Café** (see ❷) has tables inside and outside for tapas and snacks or a full meal. There are lots of places around here touting for your custom, some better than others.

PLAZA DE ARMAS

Take the southwest exit out of the plaza one block along San Ignacio, turn left along O'Reilly and in two blocks you reach the **Plaza de Armas** ❼, the oldest square in the city. In the center of the leafy square is a statue of Carlos Manuel de Céspedes, leader of the first War of Independence, and round the edge is a small, second-hand book market. On the west side is the magnificent, baroque **Palacio de los Capitanes Generales**, dating from 1780. It was the Spanish Governor's residence until independence and then occupied by Cuban Presidents until they moved to the Capitolio and it became the mayor's office. It now houses the **Museo de la Ciudad** (Tue–Sun 9.30am–5pm; charge), filled with colonial artifacts and best seen with a guided tour.

On the north side of the plaza is the **Palacio del Segundo Cabo**, the former home of the colonial Vice-Governor, but currently under renovation. Behind it stands the **Castillo de la Real Fuerza** (Tue–Sun 9.30am–5pm; charge), the oldest building in Havana, constructed in 1558 and 1577 after the city was sacked by French pirates in 1555. It is a powerful fortress, long and squat, with drawbridges, cannon and moat. On top of its tower is the city's symbol, the bronze figure of **La Giraldilla de la Habana**, commemorating the wife of conquistador Hernando de Soto who went off to Florida to search for the fountain of youth. Instead he found only a miserable death. La Giraldilla spent every afternoon in the tower watching for his return, in vain.

On the east side of the plaza is **El Templete**, a Doric-style temple with three large paintings inside by Jean-Baptiste Vermay. A column marks the spot where the city was refounded in 1519, with a Mass being said under the ceiba tree. Nearby stands the beautiful **Hotel Santa Isabel**, built in the 18th century as the **Palacio del Conde de Santovenia**.

PLAZA DE SAN FRANCISCO

Exit at the southwest corner, heading west along Obispo, the first street in

Flower girls   *Plaza Vieja*

the old city to be pedestrianized and restored. It is also one of the busiest. Turn left at the corner with Mercaderes, where you pass the **Hotel Ambos Mundos**. It was here that Ernest Hemingway wrote *For Whom the Bell Tolls* and you can visit his room. On the next corner, with Obrapía, is the yellow **Casa de la Obra Pía** (Tue–Sat 9.30am–4.30pm; donations welcome), built in 1665. The imposing doorway leads into a creeper-strewn courtyard of a fine mansion, now a furniture museum.

Walk east along Obrapía until you get to the waterfront, then turn right past the **Diana Garden**, commemorating the life of Diana, Princess of Wales, and the **Lonja de Comercio**, a former commodities market, to reach the **Plaza de San Francisco** ❽. The highlight here is the old **Convento de San Francisco de Asís** with its bell tower once used as a lookout for pirates. It was used by the British in 1762–3 for Protestant services and after that the Catholics refused to worship there. A museum of religious art occupies the cloisters and the Basílica Menor is used as a concert hall for classical recitals, often held in the early evening.

PLAZA VIEJA

One block west along Teniente Rey brings you to the charming and beautifully restored **Plaza Vieja** ❾, the third open space in the city after the Plaza de Armas and Plaza de San Francisco. This 16th-century square was originally known as Plaza Nueva and was always residential with no military, religious, or administrative buildings. In the 18th century it was a market place and had a variety of names until being called Plaza Vieja in the 20th century. Batista almost destroyed it by building an underground parking lot in 1952 and the surrounding buildings crumbled. Now beautifully restored, it has come back to life with museums, art galleries, cafés, restaurants, and bars. In the southwest corner is the **Cervecería La Muralla**, inside the Factoría Plaza Vieja (see ❸), a microbrewery offering cold beer as a pit stop.

Anyone interested in the history of rum on the island should then head east a couple of blocks to the waterfront and turn south for the **Museo del Ron** ❿ (Avenida del Puerto 262 e/ Sol y Muralla; Mon–Thu 9am–5pm, Fri–Sun 9am–4pm; charge, guide and drink included). The tour takes you through the whole process of rum production but the highlight for many people is the extensive model railroad running around a model sugar refinery. There is an adjoining Havana Club bar and a shop.

If you have any energy left, follow the coastal road south until you reach the old San Francisco de Paula church. Cross the road for **Almacenes San José** ⓫ (daily 10am–6pm), a converted warehouse on the water-

The covered Almacenes San José, perfect for souvenir-shopping

front containing Havana's largest art and craft market, the perfect place to browse for souvenirs. There is even a Cadeca for currency exchange. Another old warehouse next door, the **Antiguo Almacén de la Madera y el Tabaco** (see ❹), is now a microbrewery (*cervecería*) and restaurant overlooking the harbor, a welcome respite at the end of the long walk.

Food and Drink

❶ BIANCHINI

San Ignacio 68, Callejón del Chorro, Plaza de la Catedral; second location at Sol 12 e/ Oficios y Avenida del Puerto, near the Museo del Ron; http://dulceria-bianchini.com; daily 9am–9pm; $

A cosy coffee shop offering snacks and light lunches with everything homemade. Kathia, the Swiss-Italian owner, has stamped her personality on the décor and the food quality. The quiches are tasty, the croissants flaky, and the cakes divine. The coffee is all locally grown and roasted and the chocolate is organic, from Baracoa.

❷ ESTO NO ES UN CAFÉ

San Ignacio 58, Callejón del Chorro, Plaza de la Catedral; tel: 7-862 5109; daily noon–midnight; $$

This small, arty tapas bar and restaurant is worth seeking out. The delicious Cuban food is beautifully and humorously presented with a modern twist, accompanied by great cocktails, bottled beer, or wine by the glass. There is usually a set-price dish of the day, which comes with a drink beforehand, a glass of wine with your meal, bread and butter and coffee or tea afterwards. Or choose à la carte.

❸ CERVECERÍA LA MURALLA

Factoría Plaza Vieja, San Ignacio esq Muralla; tel: 7-866 4433; daily noon–midnight; $$

This is a state-run microbrewery, so the service is awful and the food average at best, but it is still a lovely location in Plaza Vieja, with wrought-iron tables and chairs outside or inside seating. Order a meter of beer to share – it comes in a tube with ice down the middle – and relax to soak up the ambience while a live band plays.

❹ ANTIGUO ALMACÉN DE LA MADERA Y EL TABACO

Avenida del Puerto esq Paula; daily noon–midnight; $$

This vast old waterfront warehouse for timber and tobacco has been converted into a microbrewery and restaurant, conveniently next to Almacenes San José, so when you've finished your shopping for souvenirs, you can take the weight off your feet with a cold beer. There are tables outside overlooking the water, or in the barn with a view of the brewing machinery where a band plays to take your mind off the slow service and indifferent food. Check your bill.

Cementerio de Colón

VEDADO WALKING TOUR

Vedado is an elegant residential area, built on sugar wealth from the mid-19th century onwards but, like most of Havana, is now crumbling for lack of maintenance. Its residents, however, make this the most vibrant district for eating, drinking, nightlife, and the arts – not to be missed.

DISTANCE: 3 miles (4.8 km) of walking
TIME: A full day
START: Cementerio de Colón
END: Hotel Nacional
POINTS TO NOTE: Take a taxi to the cemetery as it is quite remote. Take precautions against the sun as there is little shade and it is best to go in the morning before it gets too hot.

Vedado's heyday was the first half of the 20th century, when Cuba supplied the US with all its sugar needs and revenues poured back into the island. Beautiful mansions and villas, as well as more modest but still opulent family homes, were built along broad avenues and leafy streets. US tourists, film stars, and the mafia mob, attracted by rum, gambling, and sex, brought excitement and nightlife. Luxurious hotels were built with laundered money and housed glitzy casinos and cabarets.

Today Vedado has an air of faded grandeur. The casinos and brothels were eliminated after the Revolution, but this is still the place to come for nightlife. Midnight hums to a Latin beat, but you are less likely to hear traditional Cuban music than jazz, while young Cubans listen to rap, hip hop, rock, and reggaeton.

CEMENTERIO DE COLÓN

The **Cementerio de Colón** ❶ (Columbus Cemetery; entrance on Calzada de Zapata; tel: 7-830 4517; daily 8am–5pm; guided tour) is one of the largest necropolises in the world, at 140 acres (57 hectares). Work began in the 1860s, after a competition for its design was won by a Spaniard, Calixto de Loira y Cardosa, who ensured the dead could be separated by social status. He died before it was completed in 1876 and became one of the first to be buried here.

The wealthy competed to create the most impressive tombs and the result is a forest of Grecian temples and columns, crucified Christs and angels of mercy; an eclectic mix of Gothic and new-classical styles. It is well worth paying for a tour as your guide will bring to life the history and legends of the

famous people interred there, or you can get a map from the office on the left as you go in.

PLAZA DE LA REVOLUCIÓN

From the entrance to the cemetery, head east along Calzada de Zapata, before turning right, southeast, along the Paseo, the major thoroughfare running from the Malecón to the **Plaza de la Revolución ❷**. This is the governmental heart of modern Havana: a vast, bleak square, big enough to hold the masses that came to hear Fidel's famous eight-hour May Day speeches, but normally empty of anyone except tourists and taxis.

Despite the Soviet-style monolithic architecture, most of the buildings went up during Batista's time, when the dictator expressed his taste for intimidating, uninspired design, as seen in the gray former **Justice Ministry**, finished in 1958, that now houses the Central Committee of the Communist Party. The **Ministerio del Interior**, Cuba's most sinister and secretive organization, is in Cuba's most photographed building, because of the giant mural of Che Guevara executed in black metal attached to the outside. Other buildings include the **Palacio de la Revolución**, where senior ministers have their offices (no photography allowed), the **Biblioteca Nacional** and the **Television and Radio Information and Communications Building**.

At the center is the mighty **Monumento José Martí** (Mon–Sat 9.30am–4.30pm; charge), which houses an informative museum, including the original designs for the plaza. You can go up the monument for an impressive 360-degree view of the city.

On the northeast corner is the **Teatro Nacional de Cuba**, a modern building dating from 1979 containing two auditoriums (Sala Covarrubias and Sala Avellaneda, together holding 3,500 people), the lively **Café Cantante Mi Habana**, a piano bar and a large sculpture garden exhibiting works by Cuban artists. High-quality performances of ballet, opera, drama, concerts, and musicals are held here.

UNIVERSIDAD DE LA HABANA

Leave the Plaza de la Revolución heading northeast past the Teatro Nacional and the Interior Ministry along Avenida Carlos M de Céspedes. At the major junction with Avenida de los Presidentes and Avenida Salvador Allende (also called Carlos III), keep straight on, along Zapata/Zanja with the **Quinta de los Molinos** on your right. This was the site of 18th-century snuff mills and the gardens were popular in colonial times, although they are now neglected. On the east side is **La Madriguera**, a center for young artists and musicians, where you might hear rehearsals in passing of rap, hip hop, rumba, or more traditional Cuban rhythms.

The murals of revolutionaries Che Guevara and Camilo Cienfuegos on Plaza de la Revolución

Friendly smile at Coppelia

Take a left turn past the sports stadium along Aguirre to the **Universidad de La Habana ❸**, a lovely group of classical buildings in golden stone placed around a cool and leafy garden, reached by climbing an impressive flight of steps at the head of San Lázaro. Opposite the staircase is a stark **monument to Julio Antonio Mella**, containing the ashes of the student who founded the Cuban Communist Party and was assassinated in Mexico in 1929.

In the Faculty of Biology lies the **Museo Antropológico Montané** (Felipe Poey Building, Plaza Ignacio Agramonte; Mon–Fri 9am–noon, 1–4pm), with an excellent collection of pre-Columbian artifacts including the famous wooden Taíno tobacco idol, dating from around the 12th century, found in Maisí, at the far eastern tip of Cuba. There is also the **Museo Napoleónico** (San Miguel 1159 esq Ronda; Tue–Sat 9.30am–5pm, Sun 9.30am–noon), housed in a delightful mansion with a small garden. Much of this unexpected collection of Napoleonic art and memorabilia was brought by Julio Lobo, a 19th-century politician and sugar baron, from his travels in Europe. It includes Napoleon's death mask and a fine library.

By this stage you might be in need of sustenance and a late lunch. There are plenty of places to eat around the university, but just along San Lázaro, near the university steps is **Locos por Cuba** (see ❶), a good value *paladar* serving sound Cuban dishes at reasonable prices. For a more upmarket ambience, walk north along L to **Cibo Café** (see ❷), where the menu is more Italian and international, but still economical.

LA RAMPA

Avenida L runs northwest from the university for a couple of blocks where it intersects with Calle 23, known as La Rampa. This is one of the main arteries of Vedado, running roughly east – west from the Malecón to the cemetery. Several airlines have their offices here, there is the International Press Center, hotels, nightclubs, cinema, an excellent jazz club, and a whole host of snack bars.

On the corner of L with La Rampa is the iconic **Hotel Habana Libre ❹**. Built during the dictatorship and inaugurated three months before Batista fled as the Havana Hilton, it became Castro's headquarters for several months in 1959, with his embryonic government taking over an entire floor. The café was the scene of a famous poison attempt on Castro, who used to spend late nights here chatting to kitchen staff. The cyanide capsule intended for his chocolate milkshake broke in the freezer. Over the years, refurbishments have replaced the atmospheric 1950s interior with a bland, modern design.

Opposite the hotel on the other side of La Rampa is the **Coppelia Ice Cream Park ❺**. This ice cream palace was built to replace the notoriously elitist Vedado ice cream parlors. The domed building,

Havana University   *The view from the Hotel Nacional*

occupying a whole block, was designed by Mario Girona in 1966, based on an idea by Celia Sánchez, friend and companion of Fidel Castro and heroine of the Sierra Maestra campaign. It was in the park that the opening scenes of the 1994 movie *Fresa y Chocolate* were filmed. The title refers to the two most common flavors, sometimes the only ones available, strawberry and chocolate. Tourists can wait for two hours or more with everyone else if they wish to buy ice cream and pay in *moneda nacional*, but it is quicker (and more expensive) to pay in CUC$ at one of the stands on the fringes of the park. The ice cream is not as good as it used to be and there are usually shortages.

The architecturally elegant Art Deco **Hotel Nacional de Cuba** ❻ marks the end of La Rampa at the Malecón, although the entrance is on Avenida O esq Calle 21. Perched on a bluff, the hotel dates from 1930 and still has an air of faded grandeur about it, with its vintage Otis high-speed elevators, magnificent reception, and old cannon in the gardens overlooking the sea. It is now a National Monument and certainly a landmark in Vedado. A host of famous people have stayed here, including Sir Winston Churchill, Frank Sinatra, and Ava Gardner. Have a look round and then head out into the garden for a sit down and a drink (see ❸).

Food and Drink

❶ LOCOS POR CUBA
San Lázaro 1203 Altos e/ Mazón y Basarrate; tel: 7-873 8182; noon–midnight; $$
A good-value and locally popular *paladar* serving sound Cuban dishes at reasonable prices. You can get one of the small tables on the balcony overlooking the street, or indoors in the shade. The emphasis is on pork, but they serve a good *ropa vieja*, and there is chicken, fish, or pizza, all traditionally presented with rice and vegetables.

❷ CIBO CAFÉ
L 452 apto 1 esq 25; tel: 5-406 2416; noon–midnight; $$
Smart black and white décor in this apartment *paladar*, where the huge windows are thrown open to catch the breeze. Pizza, pasta, and other Italian dishes are nicely presented, but you can also get a sandwich and or a vegetarian option.

❸ HOTEL NACIONAL DE CUBA
O esq 21; T7-873 3564; $
An excellent place to end your walk with a sundowner cocktail in the garden looking towards Old Havana. From here you have a great view of the old cars spluttering their way along the seafront drive, outflanked by the gleaming, open-topped restorations taking tourists on a sunset excursion along the coast. You can also while away some time here until you head off night-time entertainment.

The green hills of the Sierra del Rosario

SIERRA DEL ROSARIO

Within easy reach of Havana, the Sierra del Rosario is the perfect antidote to the city. Lush green forests cover the steep hillsides providing a habitat for birds, butterflies, orchids, and other natural beauties and much of the Sierra has been declared a Unesco Biosphere Reserve.

DISTANCE: 120 miles (192 km)

TIME: A full day

START: Havana

END: Havana

POINTS TO NOTE: Take a swimsuit, suntan lotion, a sun hat, and sunglasses. There are lots of tours available with guides or, to avoid large groups, take a taxi or hire a car. This excursion can be combined with Viñales for an overnight stay and you can arrange for your driver to pick you up the next day or return to Havana by bus.

A six-lane, relatively quiet, *autopista* runs west from Havana as far as Pinar del Río, 110 miles (178 km) away. There are also the Carretera Norte, which runs along the northern coast, and the Carretera Central, the old main road to the west which runs through smaller towns where the traffic is slow. It doesn't take long for the scenery to become rural and as you get further from Havana, the mountain range of the Sierra del Rosario looms ahead of you.

LAS TERRAZAS

After about 45 minutes' drive, turn off the *autopista* at Km 51 to **Las Terrazas** ❶ (charge), which is 2.4 miles (3.8 km) to the north. In 1967 the government built a colony here, on 12,300 acres (5,000 ha) of land, in an attempt to assist the rural community after indiscriminate logging had all but denuded the countryside. The terraces were created to help prevent further soil erosion. Now run as a tourist complex on principles of sustainable development, the little colony flourishes, its forested terraces tumbling down to a long artificial lake where a café perches on a pier over the water. There is even a zip line, called a canopy tour, across the lake into the trees. The community is the base for several artists who sell crafts and paintings from their workshops and there is a museum of pre-Columbian artifacts where you can often hear music.

At the **Eco-Center** (Centro de Investigaciones Ecológicas) you can hire guides who specialize in the forest's flora and birdlife and will lead you on for-

Orquideario blooms

Orquideario sign

est trails. The **San Juan River Trail** ends at the fabulous **Baños de San Juan** where you can bathe in a deep mountain pool fed by a waterfall. Another lovely trail leads to the partly-restored **Buenavista** coffee plantation, one of several in the area. There are a couple of nice places for lunch in Las Terrazas, including a rare vegetarian restaurant, **El Romero** (see ❶), but whatever time of day you are here, you must try the coffee. The best is at **Café de María** (see ❷), in an unprepossessing location in an apartment block, where you can have it hot and strong or iced with a liqueur. If you want to stay overnight, there is the government-run **Hotel Moka**, or a few *casas particulares* outside the park on the road to Cayajabos.

SOROA

Soroa ❷ can be reached either by returning to the *autopista* and then turning off again, or by a winding road west through the mountains about 11 miles (18 km), then at the junction turning southeast. You will pass the recently renovated small hotel, **Castillo en las Nubes** (see ❸), which is a lovely place to stop for refreshment. Perched on a hillside, there are lovely views and a small swimming pool.

Soroa is best known for its **Jardín Botánico Orquideario Soroa** (tel: 48-523 871; 8.30am–4.30 pm; charge, guided tours), a hillside tropical garden containing some 700 types of orchid, more than 200 of them indigenous, and most of them in flower between December and March. There is a display of blooming orchids at any time of year, but winter is the best time to see them flowering among the other plants and trees in the garden. The path winds gently uphill, with rest stops, and there is a lovely view from the top.

If you are hot after your walk, which can be very humid, you can cool off in the **Salto de Soroa**, the local waterfall, which plunges 66 feet (20 m) into a rocky pool. The

Bathing in the Salto de Soroa

entrance is opposite the Orquideario, although the waterfall is some distance away down a mostly-paved track. The trail is beautiful even if there isn't much water in the river in the dry season, as you can see birds, butterflies, lizards, and lots of plants. Wear shoes with a good grip, as the rock pools can be slippery. Sometimes the falls are closed for lack of rainfall to feed the waterfall.

A dirt path climbs from the base of the waterfall to the **Mirador de Venus** at the top of the hill, from where you can enjoy a panoramic view of the mountains and the plains running to the coast. It is a steep path of less than a mile, but if you can't manage it, there are horses to rent. After your hike you might enjoy a massage at the **Baños Romanos** (9am–4pm; charge) at the entrance to the Salto.

You have the option to carry on along the *autopista* to Pinar del Río, then turning north to Viñales for the night. If you are returning to Havana, however, an alternative route is to follow the Carretera Central, joining it at Candelaria and traveling through Artemisa, Guanajay, and Bauta.

Food and Drink

① EL ROMERO
Las Terrazas; tel: 48-578 555; 9am–10pm; $$
A rare thing in Cuba, this is a vegetarian restaurant serving imaginative and varied food, with all the ingredients locally sourced and organic. It is in the residential area of Las Terrazas, in a villa with tables inside or on the veranda with a lovely view of the colony. Make a reservation if you can, because tour parties often take over the place and then quality and service suffer.

② CAFÉ DE MARÍA
Las Terrazas; 9am–10pm; $
Located in an apartment block with a small balcony overlooking the colony, this is the place to come for some of the best coffee in Cuba. Locally grown, roasted and ground, you can try it hot and strong or iced and creamy with a liqueur to add a different flavor. The late María ran this café for 40 years, and has been succeeded by her family. Fame means that it is often crowded with tour parties, but try and get a seat on the balcony for a lovely view. Coffee beans are also for sale.

③ CASTILLO EN LAS NUBES
Carretera de Soroa Km 8; tel: 48-523 534; $$
About a mile uphill up a rough road from the orchidarium, this newly renovated boutique hotel on top of El Fuerte hill has a look of a fortified mansion about it. Built as a holiday home in the 1940s, it was abandoned after the Revolution. In the 1970s it was opened as a restaurant but fell into disrepair until it recently reopened as a hotel with 6 rooms. Get a table by the window for a *criollo* meal or just take a drink onto the terrace for the expansive views all the way to the southern coast.

The verdant and fertile Viñales Valley

VIÑALES

Stunningly picturesque, the Viñales Valley is a photographer's dream. The red soil, tilled by oxen, contrasts with the vibrant green of the palm trees in the fields and the flat-topped, sheer-sided mountains, known as mogotes, which are often shrouded in mist at dawn and cast long shadows at dusk.

DISTANCE: 78 miles (125 km)
TIME: A full day
START: Viñales
END: Viñales
POINTS TO NOTE: Viñales can be reached by bus from Havana via Pinar del Río and there are lots of *casas particulares* where you can stay. However, reservations are essential in high season as everywhere fills up. For the tour, hire a car or taxi for the day. *Taxi collectivos* (old US station wagons) run from Viñales to Cayo Jutías, 1 hour 40 mins – 2 hours, but do not stop at other attractions. Take a swimsuit and towel for the trip to the beach and lots of sun protection and insect repellent. Taking a picnic is recommended.

The Viñales Valley lies in the Sierra de los Órganos, a region protected as the Parque Nacional de Viñales and dominated by the bizarre *mogotes*, fists of hard limestone that were left behind when the softer rock around them eroded over millions of years. In the Jurassic period the *mogotes* were the pillars of vast caves that subsequently collapsed; today, covered by luxuriant foliage, they have the air of overgrown ruins.

VIÑALES

The small town of **Viñales ❶** is a pleasant, rural place, where colorfully painted, single-story houses with porches line the straight streets. Many of the house owners have added extra rooms to cope with tourist demand and there are now over 500 registered *casas particulares*. There is little of architectural or historical interest in the town, which was badly hit by a hurricane in 2008, but it is relaxed and friendly. If you arrive by bus, you will be dropped off opposite the plaza on the main street, Salvador Cisneros. As well as the church, there is a Casa de la Cultura with an art gallery on the plaza and always plenty of people, as this is the local Wi-Fi hot spot, just around the corner from the telephone office, Etecsa. Heading west along the street there is a little Museo Municipal (No. 115) in the house of local War of

Farmer and his oxen

Independence heroine, Adela Azcuy (1861–1914).

A good way to get to know the area is to take the little tourist bus that runs from the plaza (8.30am–6pm, 40 mins round trip; charge) to the two hotels outside town on the way to Pinar del Río: **Los Jazmines** and **La Ermita**. It is a hop-on/hop-off service, so you can get off to explore if you want to. Both hotels enjoy fabulous views over the valley, with its tobacco fields and *mogotes* and it is pleasant to while away some time on the terrace with a coffee or cold drink enjoying the peaceful vista. The latter is only 20 minutes' walk from town if you want to return on foot.

There are plenty of trails around Viñales and you can explore on your own or go with a guide recommended by your *casa* owner. Guides will take you on foot, horse or bicycle to visit farms and other local attractions, but be aware that every stop will probably involve parting with some money to buy drinks, locally-made cigars, honey, or coffee from the farmers. The rich red soil is perfect for tobacco growing and you will see the steep-roofed *secaderos*, sheds in which tobacco is dried and the small homesteads where farming families live. Most of the farmers here grow a mixture of tobacco, maize, bananas, and pineapples, all on a small scale, and most keep a pig and some chickens, as well as working oxen and horses. In the fields, simple wooden or iron plows are pulled by these placid oxen (*bueyes*), rather than tractors, and are often used to pull carts as well.

To get further afield, hire a car or taxi for the day. Again, your *casa* owner can recommend a driver who may be an informative guide along the way.

WEST OF VIÑALES

The **Mural de la Prehistoria ❷**, an enormous, garish painting that covers the flank of the Dos Hermanas *mogote*, about 2 miles (3 km) west of Viñales, was commissioned by Fidel Castro in

Mural de la Prehistoria　　　　　*Tending the crops at a tobacco plantation*

the 1960s to portray the emergence of Socialist Man from the primal wilderness. One of Diego de Rivera's students, Leovigildo González, took on the commission, directing dozens of local painters. It is regularly touched up by artists who dangle precariously from the cliff top on rope swings, but is generally considered a monstrous piece of graffiti. More enjoyable is the zip line, **Loma de Fortín Canopy Tour** (3 miles/5.5 km from Viñales; charge), which runs for 0.6 miles (1.1 km) between eight elevated platforms from the *mogotes*, over tobacco fields and across the valley.

Continue heading southwest and at the village of La Moncada, 11 miles (18 km) from Viñales, is the **Gran Caverna de Santo Tomás** ❸ (daily 9am–5pm; 90-minute guided tour; charge). This is said to be Cuba's largest cave system, with some 28.5 miles (46 km) of tunnels and passages, although you are only shown a small part, with some lovely stalactites. Hard hats and lamps are provided.

NORTH COAST

Follow the very pot-holed and slow road from La Moncada through Pons and the former copper mining center of Minas de Matahambre to **Cayo Jutías** ❹ on the north coast near Santa Lucía. A long causeway through the mangroves connects the 4.2-mile (6.7-km) cay to the mainland and this is a lovely beach

excursion, where the sand is white and the sea is turquoise and clear. The water is quite shallow with lots of sea grass for some distance, but further out there is a reef for snorkeling. The cay is uninhabited, there is no hotel, just a couple of rustic restaurants on the sand for unremarkable food and drink and appalling service until 6pm. However, the area by the beach bars can get busy with tour parties, so for peace and quiet walk further along the 1.8-mile (3-km) beach towards the lighthouse. Expect mangroves, driftwood, and some seaweed

Cayo Jutías lighthouse

A cigar roller at work

Cuban cigars

Thanks to the ideal climate and soil, plus centuries of expertise in cultivating tobacco, Cuba produces arguably the world's finest cigars. The big fat Cuban cigar holds as important a role in the national identity as rum and salsa. The most highly prized tobacco comes from the *vegas* (plantations) around the town of San Juan y Martínez and San Luís in the western province of Pinar del Río, in an area called the Vuelta Abajo. It is this region's leaves – the most important of which are grown under cheesecloth to protect them from direct sunlight – that are made into world-famous brands such as Cohiba, Montecristo and Romeo y Julieta. Around 100 million cigars are exported each year and the industry is an important hard-currency earner.

In order to stamp out the black market in counterfeit cigars, official cigar boxes bear a holographic seal. A box bought on the street may look like the real thing, with the packaging and cigar bands pilfered from a factory, but the tobacco will be inferior. It's best to buy from an official shop where prices are higher but the cigars are genuine. If you get the chance to inspect the contents of a box before you buy, check that the cigars are of a similar color (the darker they are, the stronger the flavor) and that if you squeeze them they readily spring back into shape and don't crackle.

on the sand, but it is beautiful. Taking a picnic is recommended. Sun beds, umbrellas, pedalos, kayaks, snorkels, towels, and other equipment can be hired by the beach bars.

Return along the causeway to Santa Lucía, then head east along the coast for 23 km to San Cayetano on the road to La Palma. The road is in very poor condition but offers a circular route by joining the road running from Viñales to Puerto Esperanza, a fishing town. At San Cayetano, turn southeast for 10 km, then south to Viñales.

NORTH OF VIÑALES

You will pass the **Cueva del Indio** ❺ (daily 10am–5.30pm; 25-minute tours) in manicured grounds amid towering rocks. It is called the Indian Cave because the indigenous Guanahatabey people used it as a cemetery and refuge during the Spanish conquest. You climb steps to the cave then follow a contorted limestone tunnel down to an underground lake, on which you take a short boat trip as part of the tour. It is on every tourist itinerary and as such, you can expect long queues at any time of day. However, it is a pleasant rural location, there is a restaurant and bar, and handicraft stalls, although there is a better, private restaurant across the road: **Paladar La Pimienta** (see ❶), and several others in the area.

A couple of miles further on the Viñales road is the **Cueva de San**

Entering the Cueva del Indio

Miguel ⑥, a small cave with a bar at the entrance, through which you walk to reach **El Palenque de los Cimarrones**, a bar, restaurant, and museum (noon–4pm). The cave was first used by Amerindians as shelter and later by runaway slaves. The museum is a reconstruction of the slaves' settlement, with a few cooking utensils and little else. In the afternoons the restaurant is full of tour parties. On Saturday nights, the bar at the entrance has music and dancing and is a popular nightspot for locals.

From here it is only a couple of miles back to Viñales, passing the **Jardín Botánico** (daylight hours; donation appreciated) at the east end of Salvador Cisneros, almost opposite the gas station. First planted in the 1930s and maintained by the same family ever since, this pretty little garden has a wide selection of flowers and fruits and there is usually a selection of seasonal produce for you to try.

At the junction by the gas station, turn left on to the road to the Cemetery for about a mile to the **Finca Agroecológica el Paraíso** (see ②), an organic farm in the National Park. The farmer can give you a tour of his vegetable beds if you are interested, but the restaurant is the great attraction here. Not only is the food fresh and tasty, but you can also while away some time admiring the view of the *mogotes* with a house cocktail in your hand, perfect at the end of a long day on the road. Then stay for dinner.

Food and Drink

① PALADAR LA PIMIENTA

Cueva del Indio, Valle de Viñales; tel: 5-818 8875; $$

A decent *paladar* which makes a pleasant stop before or after visiting the Cueva del Indio. Set back off the road along a path, the tables are under a thatched roof (*palapa*) and you look out over a tranquil, rural scene with grazing farm animals. Typical *comida criolla*, where you choose your meat and it comes with all the usual accompaniments in abundance. There are several *paladares* in this area to choose from.

② FINCA AGROECOLÓGICA EL PARAÍSO

Carretera al Cementerio Km 1.5; tel: 5-818 8581; $$

An excellent place to try traditional Cuban cuisine, with all the produce organic and grown right outside the door. Food is served family style, with bowls of seasonal vegetables, salads, meat, rice and beans filling the tables. It is great for lunch or dinner, but also wonderful in the late afternoon, when you can relax with a cocktail and admire the view across the vegetable garden to the *mogotes* beyond as the light turns honey-colored before sunset. Take a flashlight if you are walking back to town after dark.

Playa Girón is much more tranquil these days

THE ZAPATA PENINSULA

The best known of Cuba's wildlife havens, the Zapata peninsula is a refuge for many bird and animal species, but earned a place in history when the unsuccessful 1961 Bay of Pigs invasion was repulsed at Playa Girón.

DISTANCE: 35 miles (56 km)
TIME: One-and-a-half days
START: Playa Larga
END: Playa Girón
POINTS TO NOTE: Birdwatching tours start early in the morning, so it is best to get to the area the day before to arrange a guide (obligatory in the National Park). Go to the office of the Parque Nacional Ciénaga de Zapata (Playa Larga; tel: 45-987 249; daily 8am–4.30pm). If you want to scuba dive as well, allow an extra day or two. Bring suntan lotion, insect repellent, binoculars, hat, and sunglasses. Always carry water with you. There is a limited bus service from Havana but it is better to hire a car as birdwatching guides do not offer transport. December–April is the driest time of year, so best for getting around the swamp, and there are more birds, with migrating birds resting here.

The whole peninsula is a Unesco Biosphere Reserve, the Gran Parque Natural Montemar, or the Parque Nacional Ciénaga de Zapata. Most of the peninsula is barely above sea level and is flooded every year during the rainy season (June–October). About 30 percent is slightly higher, supporting a wide strip of forest some 10 miles (16 km) from the southern coastline.

Narrow canals connect lagoons with the surrounding shallow seas. These were excavated by hand over the centuries to facilitate lumber transportation. Regrettably, the peninsula's virgin hardwood forest has been thoroughly exploited and even the tallest trees today are only secondary growth. Much of the swamp is covered with a thick mat of peat, which acts as a gigantic mattress during the dry season. There are many hidden sinkholes and caverns in the underlying hard sediment of limestone.

PLAYA LARGA

Playa Larga ❶ is a small, scruffy town on the coast at the head of the Bahía

The southern half of Matanzas province is mainly low, marshy terrain, a haven for wildlife on land and in the water.

The endangered Cuban parakeet

de Cochinos, commonly known as the Bay of Pigs. There is a basic hotel and several *casas particulares* as well as a few private restaurants. The beach is sandy, pleasant and there are dive sites just offshore. On arrival, you will want to find your accommodation, arrange an early-morning birdwatching tour for the next day at the National Parks office and then have lunch. There are several good *paladares*, including **Chef Orlando** (see ❶), on the left as you head out of town towards the north.

NORTH OF PLAYA LARGA

After lunch, drive north for ten minutes to the crocodile farm, **Criadero de Cocodrilos** ❷ (Guamá; tel: 45-913 224; daily 9am–5pm; charge). This is a regular stop for tour parties, but interesting to see

how the endemic Cuban crocodile, the Rhombifer, has been saved from extinction. Thousands have been successfully released into the wild to restore the native population, but the majority end up as skins for shoes and bags, while their meat is eaten. It tastes a bit like fishy pork and can be very chewy. At the farm the animals are grouped by size and age and visitors are shown a selection, from babies of 5–10 months old which you can hold, to fully grown adults. Some crocodiles live to be 100 years old.

Just down the road, at **La Boca de Guamá**, boats carry passengers through a canal to the **Laguna del Tesoro** ❸ (Treasure Lagoon; every 30 minutes, 9am–6pm, minimum 8 people, return after 1 hour; charge). The lake got its name because, it was said, indigenous Taíno people of the area threw all their

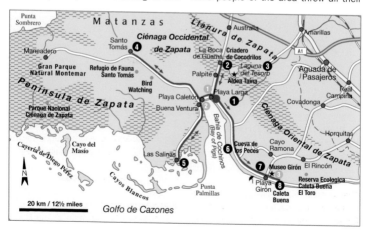

valuables into it rather than surrender them to the Spanish. There's a romanticized mock Taíno village, **Aldea Taína**,

The Bay of Pigs

The Bay of Pigs battle began shortly after midnight on April 17, 1961, when the 2506th assault brigade – a CIA-trained force of some 1,500 mercenaries and Cuban exiles – landed to force the overthrow of Fidel. However, El Jefe Máximo was ready for them with Soviet-built T-34 tanks and a few T-33 fighter jets, and, after two days of intense air and land battles, the 2506th surrendered. Of the invading force, 107 were killed and 1,189 were taken prisoner. Most were later released back to the US in return for a US$53-million consignment of medicines and foodstuffs. Castro, who led the people's militia in the battle, lost 161 men and women (five of these were civilians). The Museo de Girón was built at the landing site to commemorate the events. Outside, you can inspect a couple of tanks used in the defense. Inside are two rooms full of documents, photos, and weapons and an array of artifacts, among them a 12.7mm anti-aircraft battery used against US planes, and a map showing the mercenaries' route from Puerto Cabezas, Nicaragua. Their invasion was preceded by an unsuccessful bombing raid on the Cuban Air Force, which put Castro on full alert. You can see a video compilation of footage from the era (in Spanish only).

and a rustic hotel, Villa Guamá, on islands in the lagoon, with life-size statues of Taínos by the sculptor, Rita Longa. Snail kites (*Rostrhamus sociabilis*) are abundant here, as are the snails on which they feed with their long, curved beaks. You will also find the endemic manjuarí (garfish or pike) – its teeth, snout and body are a crude parallel to those of a crocodile, and its lineage goes back some 70 million years. Birdwatching is good on the lagoon, best early in the morning before the tour parties arrive, which is why some people stay at the hotel.

Return to Playa Larga for drinks, dinner, and an early night, ready for an early start. Lovers of seafood won't be disappointed, but never eat turtle, which appears on menus at various restaurants from time to time, as sea turtles are endangered and protected.

Birdwatching

The next morning, set off very early with your guide into the National Park. The mixed habitat of mangrove swamp, thick scrub, forest, and saltpans attracts a wide range of birds with a total count of 190 species. Most of Cuba's endemic species can be found here: the bee hummingbird, Cuban parakeet, Gundlach's hawk, blue-headed quail dove, Cuban tody, Cuban trogon, two species of blackbird, two types of woodpecker, and a couple of very small owls. Some species, such as the Zapata wren and rail (close to extinction), are unique to the swamp.

Flamingos in flight near Playa Larga

One of the best places for ornithologists lies north of the village of **Santo Tomás** ❹, west of Playa Larga. Many migrant birds show up here from October through April, escaping the North American winter. The majority are warblers (more than 30 different species), but there are also herons, terns, and several birds of prey.

At **Las Salinas** ❺, 15 miles (25 km) southwest of Playa Larga, the scenery is spectacular: flamingos swoop across the milky, saltwater lagoons, and crocodiles meander out across the dirt road. Fly-fishing is becoming popular but only six anglers are allowed into the reserve at any one time, and must be accompanied by a guide who will navigate through the channels and flats.

Depending on what time you finish your birding tour, you could have lunch at Playa Caletón, on the way back to Playa Larga, where **Tiki Bahía de Cochinos** (see ❷) is a good waterfront option, or drive round the coast to one of the swimming spots with restaurants.

AROUND THE BAY OF PIGS

The road hugs the coast for the 30-minute drive to Playa Girón and there are several attractive places to stop for a swim or to look at the monuments to the Cuban dead of the Bay of Pigs invasion. You can also stop off at some of the beautiful sinkholes (cenotes) surrounded by forest, which are connected to the nearby sea by underwater tunnels. These flooded caverns in the limestone are full of tropical fish in all colors of the rainbow. The water is crystal clear even deep down, and surprisingly cold. You can snorkel or scuba dive in most of these cenotes, which is like swimming in an aquarium.

One very popular cenote is the **Cueva de los Peces** ❻ (Fish Cave; daily 9am–4pm; charge), which has been developed with restaurant and bar, while sun beds and snorkeling equipment are available for hire. The music can be very loud, especially at weekends, but the swimming and the fish are still lovely. There is no ladder, so you have to jump or dive in and climb out afterwards. There is an abundance of lizards too, some tame enough to feed on scraps under the tables. Swimming and snorkeling in the sea is even better than in the cenote, but water shoes are recommended for getting across the limestone rock to the water.

A bit further south is **Punta Perdiz** (11am–5pm; charge includes lunch buffet noon–3pm and open bar), where you climb down a ladder over rocks for excellent snorkeling. The local dive shop offers diving over offshore wrecks from the invasion as well as over the plentiful coral where there is a good variety of fish and other sea creatures. Again, water shoes are a good idea as there is no sandy beach.

PLAYA GIRÓN

The village of **Playa Girón** ❼ is spread out and scruffy, with an unattractive

Swimming in the clear waters of Caleta Buena

hotel, a collection of single-story concrete houses, two incongruous blocks of apartments at the junction with the road to Cienfuegos, and horses tethered everywhere. It is, however, important in Cold War history for the 1961 Bay of Pigs invasion, about which you can learn in the commemorative **Museo de Girón** (tel: 45-984 122; daily 8am-5pm, charge), see box page 52. Outside there are aircraft, tanks and boats belonging to both sides. If you are in need of refreshment, there is a bar and restaurant opposite the museum: **Bar Brig** (see ③).

Playa Girón is also popular as a dive site and there are several wrecks to explore, both old and more recent, deliberately sunk fishing vessels which have been allowed to grow new reef.

There is a dive operation at the hotel which provides gear and instructors.

Five miles (8 km) southeast of Playa Girón is **Caleta Buena** ❽ (daily 10am–5pm; charge including lunch and drinks 12.30–3pm), a lovely cove blessed with spectacular sponges and red coral, home to shoals of fish. The restaurant is perched on rocks above the pale turquoise natural pools and there is a dive center. Diving and snorkeling is excellent and there are also caves and *cenotes* in the area for divers to explore. However, if you prefer peace and quiet, you can stop anywhere along the road where there is a beach and have it all to yourself. Depending on how long you want to spend by the sea, you can stay a second night in the Bay of Pigs or carry on to Cienfuegos.

Food and Drink

① CHEF ORLANDO
Playa Larga, on the road north; tel: 45-987 540; lunch and dinner; $$
Local specialties of lobster, shrimp, fish, and crocodile, all very tasty, well-cooked and inexpensive. Owner/chef Edel Orlando and his staff are very friendly and helpful and will make sure you don't leave hungry.

② TIKI BAHÍA DE COCHINOS
Playa Caletón; tel: 45-987 285; open 10am–midnight; $$
Open-air waterfront dining on a covered rooftop overlooking all the fishing boats moored offshore. This is a lovely spot for lunch or dinner, serving the freshest of fish, lobster, and shrimp as well as the usual meat dishes such as pork and ropa vieja. The bar is well stocked, the cocktails are good, wine is available and the beer is cold.

③ BAR BRIG
Opposite the museum in Playa Girón; lunch and dinner; $$
A casual bar for drinks and meals; pleasant at any time of day. There aren't many restaurants in Playa Girón, but this one serves tasty, fresh food under a thatched roof and is a useful pit stop after visiting the museum.

Keeping in touch in Cienfuegos

CIENFUEGOS

A port city tucked safely in the Bahía de Cienfuegos with a castle at the mouth of the bay to protect it from pirates, Cienfuegos is known as the 'Pearl of the South'. Founded in 1819 by French settlers from New Orleans and Louisiana, it has a certain Parisian feel, with its parks, boulevards, and colonnades.

DISTANCE: 2.5 miles (4 km) of walking, 40 miles (64 km) driving
TIME: A full day
START: Cienfuegos
END: Cienfuegos
POINTS TO NOTE: If you don't have a car, you can get the ferry across the bay to the fortress, but you will have to time your crossing carefully as it originates and terminates in Jagua for people coming into the city to work. The Botanic Gardens can be reached by taxi, so car hire is not essential.

Although settled relatively late, Cienfuegos nevertheless grew rapidly in the 19th century because of the fertile plains surrounding it, while its natural harbor allowed exports of sugar, coffee and tobacco. A railroad built between Cienfuegos and Santa Clara, the provincial capital, in the mid-19th century, sealed its position as a major trading post. The wealthy merchants who lived here built grand edifices in a fascinating blend of styles and even modest residential buildings have lovely Art Deco friezes or other architectural decorations.

Following the Revolution, Cienfuegos received massive investment from the Soviet Union, which turned the region into a major industrial center with sugar mills, cement plants, and oil refineries. Its port, the only deep-water terminal on Cuba's south coast, is home to a sizable fishing and shrimping fleet. There were plans for a Soviet-designed nuclear power plant, but construction was only 60 percent complete when the USSR collapsed and construction was halted in 1992.

PARQUE JOSÉ MARTÍ

Most of the city's best buildings are around **Parque José Martí ❶**, the square where the first settlement was founded on April 22, 1819, under the shade of a majagua tree. A bandstand now marks the place where the tree once stood. There are statues to the city's illustrious citizens, including one to José Martí, guarded by lions, as well as a triumphal arch, inscribed with the date 20 Mayo, 1902, commemorating the birth of the Cuban Republic.

Catedral Purísima Concepción

The **Catedral Purísima Concepción**, dating from 1870, dominates the square on its east side and has an impressive, but shabby, interior, complete with marble floors. Nearby, on the north side, is the neoclassical **Teatro Tomás Terry** (officially known as the Teatro de Cienfuegos; Avenida 56, 2701, between Calles 27 and 29; tel: 43-551-772; daily 9am–5pm; charge includes guided tour), inaugurated in 1890. It was named after a rich sugar baron who arrived in Cuba as a poor Venezuelan émigré, and made a dubious fortune by buying up weak and sick slaves, nursing them back to health, and then reselling them at a profit. The ornate interior of the theater is made almost entirely of precious Cuban hardwoods with classical reliefs and nymphs providing some of the decoration. National and local performances are staged here, ranging from National Ballet productions to local comedy acts.

On the west side of the plaza, the **Casa de Cultura Benjamín Duarte**, which occupies the former **Palacio de Ferrer**, the home of a rich sugar baron, is under renovation. However, for a fee, you can go in – a fascinating experience, not only to see the beautiful building, but also to witness the craftsmanship of the restoration works. It's a fine building, dating from 1894, with a wide marble staircase and beautiful stucco work. The tower on the corner

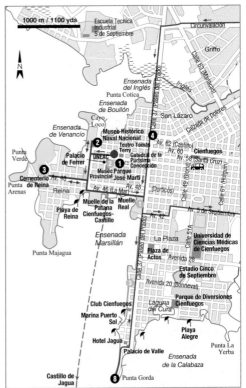

Palacio de Ferrer tower   *Cementerio de Reina graves*

was used to view shipping in the harbor. One person at a time is allowed up the wrought-iron staircase to the top of the cupula, a wonderful photo opportunity.

Next door is the UNEAC cultural center (Unión de Escritores y Artistas de Cuba – the Writers' and Artists' Union), with a pretty garden. There's a small movie theater here, an art gallery, and live bands perform on the weekend. It is a pleasant place to stop for a drink at the bar (see ①).

On the south side of the square, the **Museo Histórico Provincial** (tel: 43-519-722; Tue–Sat 10am–6pm, Sun 9am–1pm; charge) focuses on the city's role in the War of Independence, and is housed in a magnificent building which used to be the Casino Español, a cultural and political institution. The marble staircase is huge and grand and the rooms contain art and furniture as well as historical exhibits.

The streets around the Plaza José Martí hum with activity: particularly traffic-free **Boulevard San Fernando**, or Avenida 54, where food-stallholders, souvenir vendors, flower sellers, boot blacks, and other entrepreneurs ply their trades.

CAYO LOCO

Northwest of the Plaza, on a small peninsula called Cayo Loco, is the **Museo Histórico Naval Nacional** ❷ (Naval Museum; tel: 43-516-617; Tue–Sat 9am–6pm, Sun 9am–1pm; charge). To

get here, walk west along Avenida 54 for three blocks until you get to Calle 19. Turn right and head north until you see the museum, which is painted pink and white and looks like a fairy-tale castle. There is a good deal of military history here, but there are also many exhibits to do with fishing, and some archaeological and natural history items as well.

CEMENTERIO DE REINA

While on this side of town, you might also like to visit the **Cementerio de Reina** ❸ (daily 8am-5pm), which dates from 1839. Walk back down Calle 19 and then turn right, heading west along Ave 48 to the tip of the peninsula. Lovers of funerary architecture will appreciate the 19th century tombs embellished with marble and statuary. The French founders of the city are interred here, as are many soldiers who died in the Wars of Independence. The largest statue, now a National Monument, is called The Sleeping Beauty, on the tomb of a woman who died aged 24 in 1907. She carries opium plants in one hand and a poisonous snake in the other.

PASEO DEL PRADO

Return east along Ave 46, which is one block south of Ave 48. This passes the jetty from where the ferry leaves to Castillo de Jagua at the mouth of the Bay of Cienfuegos (Ave 46 entre 23 y 25, daily to the castle 8am, 1pm, 5pm, returning 6.30am, 10am, 3pm, 45 minutes,

Local hero Beny Moré on the Paseo del Prado

charge). If you do not have a car or other private transport, this is the best way of getting to the castle with fine views as you cross the bay.

Alternatively, keep walking east along Ave 48 until you come to the main street, the broad Calle 37, usually called the **Paseo del Prado** ❹ – a more fitting name for the longest boulevard in Cuba. South of Avenida 46, just before it hits the waterfront, the street is known as the Malecón. It is lined with statues (note the bronze statue of the musician and local hero Beny Moré, at the intersection of Boulevard – Ave 54 – and Prado), busts, and plaques commemorating Cienfuegos's most notable past citizens, as well as impressive colonial residences, several of which now house restaurants. A good place for lunch on the Prado is **Doña Nora** (see ❷), where there is a dining room open to the street or open air dining on the roof terrace overlooking the harbor.

AROUND CIENFUEGOS

If you have a hire car or private taxi, take Ave 42 heading east, which becomes Ave 5 de Septiembre, the road that follows the eastern side of the bay, about 2 miles (3 km) to the **Cementerio Tomás Acea** ❺ (Ave 5 de Septiembre entre Km 3 y 4, Mon–Sat 7am–6pm, free or small charge for a guide), notable for its grand replica of the Parthenon at the entrance. It is an interesting cemetery, with several ostentatious

tombs and avenues of ornamental and fruit trees.

Continue on this road around the bay, heading for Rancho Luna. East of the bridge over a narrow stretch of the bay you will find the Laguna Guanaroca, a wildlife reserve where you can see flamingos, pelicans, crabs and other wildlife. Boats with English-speaking guides take visitors out into the lagoon and through the mangroves.

CASTILLO DE JAGUA

Follow the road round the coast to Hotel Pasacaballo. You get a ferry from the here to the **Castillo Nuestra Señora de los Ángeles de Jagua** ❻ (daily 9am–4pm, charge, guides available). The fortress was built at the entrance to the bay in 1733-45 by Joseph Tantete of France to defend the area against pirate attacks, and you enter across a drawbridge over a dry moat. Inside there is an old prison, a chapel and a museum. From here you can see across the bay to the Escambray mountains beyond. Unfortunately, looking the other way, you can also see the ugly Hotel Pasacaballo on the opposite shore and the abandoned nuclear power station and housing projects of the Ciudad Nuclear (see above).

BOTANICAL GARDENS

You can not take a vehicle on the ferries either to the Hotel Pasacaballo or back

Jardín Botánico palms   *The road to Punta Gorda*

to Cienfuegos, so you have to retrace your steps back over the bridge by the lagoon. At the next junction take the right fork to San Antón, then turn left (north) on the road back to Cienfuegos. Between the villages of San Antón and Guaos is Pepito Tey, where you will find a magnificent avenue of palm trees on the right hand side of the road leading to the **Jardín Botánico de Cienfuegos** ❼, a national monument. Founded in 1901 by Edwin F Atkins, the owner of a sugar plantation, it was first a research station for the study of sugar cane, but gradually other trees and plants were added which could be used in the industry. Diversification continued and now there are areas devoted to different specializations such as medicinal plants, bamboos, fruit trees, orchids or palm trees. Try and get a guide to explain the significance of everything, as there are few signs. Return to Cienfuegos on the main road, the Circuíto Sur, which will lead you back to the Paseo del Prado.

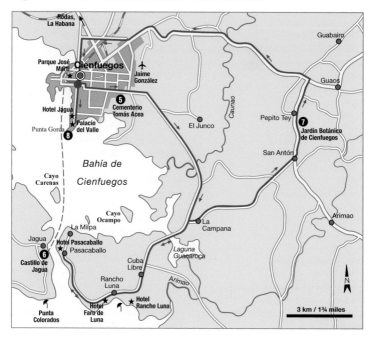

The exquisite Palacio del Valle

Food and Drink

① BAR JARDINES DE LA UNEAC (UNEAC CULTURAL CENTER)

West side of Parque José Martí, Calle 25 5411 entre 54 y 56; tel: 43-523 272; daily 9am–10pm or later for an event; $

This is a lovely courtyard garden covered with bougainvillea, a shady retreat for a cool drink at any time of day or night. There is always something going on here and at the weekends there is live music. Look at the notices on the gates for what's on.

② DOÑA NORA

Calle 37 (Prado) 4219 entre 42 y 44; tel: 43-523 331; lunch and dinner; $$

Grand marble pillars set the scene in the dining room of this elegant house which opens out onto the Prado while upstairs on the roof terrace you can enjoy open air dining looking over the harbour. There is a varied menu featuring rabbit or lamb to make a change from chicken or pork. Cocktails and live music in the evening.

③ FINCA DEL MAR

Calle 35 entre 18 y 20, Punta Gorda; tel: 43-526 598; daily 12.30pm–12.30am; $$$

This is a very elegant private restaurant, with the luxury of imported linens and furnishings from the US. It is just across the road from the waterfront and dining is open air under cover. The style of cuisine is more international than most, with good, fresh seafood, meat, and vegetarian dishes.

PUNTA GORDA

Paseo del Prado runs north-south, becoming the Malecón where it runs beside the bay. The far south is known as **Punta Gorda** ⑧, an upmarket area where wealthy families built huge houses in the first half of the 20th century. Now, there are places to stay, eat and party and it is a great spot to end your day.

The **Club Cienfuegos** (Calle 37 entre 10 y 12) was once the Cienfuegos Yacht Club where high society would come for their entertainment in the 1920s to 1950s. Painted a brilliant white, it has twin domes on the towers at the front, a balcony and a grand staircase. Today it is still an entertainment center, with tennis courts, swimming pool and playground.

The most spectacular building is **El Palacio del Valle** (at the southern end of the Malecón, daily 10am–11pm, bar 11am–2am). Built in 1894, it has an eclectic mix of architectural styles but the overall impression is of Spanish-Moorish influence, with its very ornate ceilings and other decorative work. It was designed by an Italian architect, Alfredo Colli Fanconetti, and built by Cuban, French and Arab artists and craftsmen. It was then bought by Alejandro Suero Balbín as a wedding present for his daughter on her marriage to Sr del Valle, from whom it gets its name. Now used as a bar and restaurant, it is a lovely place to have a drink on the terrace overlooking the bay and listening to live music, although there are better (private) places to eat, such as **Finca del Mar** (see ③).

Negotiating the streets of Trinidad

TRINIDAD

Trinidad is the jewel in the crown of Cuba's colonial towns and the main place outside Old Havana on any itinerary, with visitors attracted by the red-tiled roofs, pastel-colored buildings, historic mansions, cobblestone streets, and a laid-back atmosphere.

DISTANCE: 2.5–3 miles (4–5 km) of walking, 42 miles (67 km) driving
TIME: Two days
START: Trinidad
END: Trinidad
POINTS TO NOTE: The only way to explore Trinidad is on foot as many streets are closed to traffic while others are narrow and difficult to negotiate in a car. Take care with storm drains and cobbles; Trinidad is difficult for those with mobility issues. Sightseeing is best done in the morning when it is cooler, then head for the beach in the afternoon. Plan an excursion your second day. Sturdy footwear is needed for the mountains where trails are often muddy and slippery.

Trinidad has been a Unesco World Heritage Site since 1988, but was protected as a National Monument long before that. There are no garish signs or political slogans in the town itself, street lighting is low and traffic moves slowly. Most houses are single-story with huge, shuttered windows protected by metal grilles, while ancient wooden doors open to reveal cool green courtyards beyond. Only the mansions built by the rich around the Plaza Mayor are on two floors; most of these are now museums.

Outside the town, the beach at Playa Ancón is within easy reach for a few hours of relaxing, while the forested mountains of the Sierra del Escambray offer more strenuous activity and the Valley of the Sugar Mills is an historical and cultural attraction. Make sure you are back in Trinidad by sunset to enjoy the colors of the buildings bathed in a rose gold light before touring the bars and restaurants where music and dancing enliven the night.

PLAZA MAYOR

Any tour of the town will start in the splendid yet intimate **Plaza Mayor ❶**, one of Cuba's most photographed sights. All the museums and sites of interest are clustered around the square, with its magnificent palm trees, white wrought-iron benches and small statues, includ-

Picturesque street

ing two bronze greyhounds. The huge, cream-colored cathedral standing at the top of the square is the **Iglesia Parroquial de la Santísima Trinidad** (daily 10.30am for visitors, Mass daily 8pm and Sun 9am for worshippers only). Begun in 1817, it is the largest church in Cuba. It is the only church in Cuba with hand-carved Gothic altars and five aisles instead of three.

On the east side of the cathedral is a long flight of steps up to the **Casa de la Música** (second entrance on JM Márquez). This is a place to come back to at sunset, as halfway up the steps there is an open-air bar, **La Escalinata** (see ❶), where you can relax with a mojito and listen to live bands as the sun goes down and the colors of the town mellow. After dark the Casa de la Música offers live music and dancing until the early hours. The Casa also has displays of old instruments and you can buy a variety of Cuban music. At the foot of the steps east along Fernando Echerrí is the **Palenque de los Congos Reales** (see ❷), a bar open day and night where you can often catch and Afro-Cuban dance show or live music while enjoying a drink in the shady courtyard.

If you walk around the plaza in a clockwise direction from the church, you come to the former house of the Sánchez family, now the **Museo de Arquitectura Colonial** (Desengaño 83, tel: 41-993 208; Sat–Thu 9am–5pm), which tells the history of Trinidad's development, with maps and models showing how colonial craftsmen worked. Dating from 1735, the house was painted yellow rather than harsh white and when it was restored in the 1980s, sections of yellow were left as a reminder of its original color.

On the south side of the square, the attractive, balconied building contains the **Galería de Arte Universal** (Real 48; tel: 41-994 432; Fri–Wed 9am–5pm) on a site where the conquistador Hernán Cortés is said to have lived before departing for Mexico to conquer the Aztecs. Downstairs the gallery

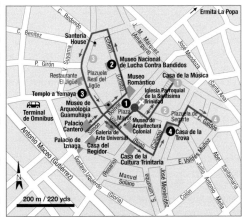

View across the rooftops   *Trinidad's cathedral*

exhibits art. Upstairs there is a shop selling arts and crafts.

If you turn left here, down Simón Bolívar, you pass several impressive colonial mansions, before reaching the **Palacio Cantero**, one of the city's most exquisite mansions, housing the **Museo Municipal de Historia** (Simón Bolívar 423; tel: 41-994 460; Sat–Thu 9am–5pm), with some fine pieces of colonial furniture and exhibits on the slave trade. There's a Roman-style bathhouse and a fountain that once spouted perfume for women and alcohol for men. However, the finest feature is the square tower, which provides an exceptional view of the whole town. Only one person at a time can go up the narrow steps, so choose a time when there aren't many visitors.

Back on the west side of the plaza, another beautiful mansion houses the **Museo de Arqueología Guamuhaya** (Simón Bolívar 457 esq Villena; tel: 41-993 420; Sat–Thu 9am–5pm). There are interesting items relating to the pre-Columbian past with developments being traced to post-Conquest times.

To the left of the cathedral is the **Museo Romántico** (Hernández 52; closed in 2017 for renovations) exhibiting period furniture and family heirlooms from the region in a sumptuous mansion. The ground floor was built in 1740 and the second floor was added at the beginning of the 19th century. In 1830–60, the Romantic period, it belonged to the Conde de Brunet, who made his money from sugar and cattle and owned 700 slaves at the time of his death.

WEST OF PLAZA MAYOR

Walk along Echerrí (Cristo) away from the Plaza Mayor and at the next junction, with P Guinart (Boca), is the old Convento de San Francisco de Asís, now the **Museo Nacional de Lucha Contra Bandidos** ❷ (tel: 41-994 121; Tue–Sun 9am–5pm). Parts of the building date from 1731, although it was enlarged and embellished in 1809. It ceased to be a convent in 1892. The displays focus on the campaign to defeat anti-Castro guerrillas in the Sierra Escambray in the 1960s. The real beauty of this building, however, is the view from the top of the bell tower. Climb the 119 granite and wooden stairs for a view of the town, the blue waters of the Caribbean and the hazy peaks of the Sierra Escambray.

Continue along Echerrí and at the next junction turn left and left again so you are on Villena (Real). A short way along is the well-known bar, **La Canchánchara** (see ❸), famous for its house cocktail of the same name, made with rum, lime, honey and sparkling water, well worth a stop.

Further along Villena on the right hand side, is the **Templo a Yemaya** ❸ (Villena 59 entre P Guinart y S Bolívar). This is an Afro-Cuban shrine where *santería* ceremonies take place and initiations are held for anyone who wants to become a *Santero*. It is open to the

Casa de la Trova is the place for live music

public and you can see dolls on the altars and symbols painted on the walls.

EAST OF PLAZAMAYOR

Carry on walking along Villena, through the Plaza Mayor, and on to the junction with Cañada. This area is pedestrianized and the streets are full of stalls selling handicrafts, mainly woodwork and crochet. Turn left along Cañada to the Plazuela de Segarte, a triangular-shaped plaza where some of the oldest houses in Trinidad are to be found. One of these is the **Casa de la Trova** ❹ (daily 9am–1am; free during the day) on your right. Built in 1717 and decorated with murals, it is popular with tourists and local people who come to enjoy the live music by day and night.

Take the northern exit from the Plazuela along José Menéndez and then turn up the Callejón de Galdós. Just up here on your left is a good place

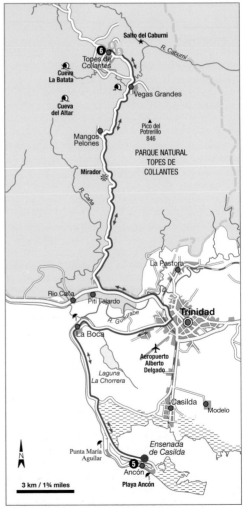

Tourist favorite Playa Ancón

Taking it easy on Playa Ancón

for lunch, **Vista Gourmet** (see ❹), an open-air restaurant which overlooks the town.

PLAYA ANCÓN

After morning's sightseeing and a good lunch, an afternoon on the beach is an attractive option. It is only some 8 miles (12 km) south of Trinidad, either by way of Casilda or the more scenic route via the small fishing village of **La Boca**, where the river meets the sea. The beach here is popular with local people and, although it is not regularly cleaned, it is quite acceptable, and the area is lively, with *casas particulares* and places to eat.

When there is plenty of demand, there is a hop-on hop-off, open-topped, double-decker tourist bus from outside Cubatur's office in Trinidad to Playa Ancón (theoretically at 9am, 11am, 2pm, return 12.30pm, 3.30pm, 6pm), or you can share a taxi. Some people prefer the flexibility of a bicycle, which is not hard work as the peninsula is flat. Tour companies and some *casas particulares* rent bikes, but check it is roadworthy. Alternatively, car hire companies will rent you a scooter for the day.

Playa Ancón ❺ is a long sandy stretch of beach with warm, clear-blue waters, and some sea grass and coral for snorkeling over. The local dive operator by the bus stop offers trips by boat for better snorkeling and diving. Bath-

ers tend to gather on the sections in front of the hotels, where they can be within easy reach of transport, sunbeds, umbrellas, food, and drink. Beach service includes *coco loco*, a fresh coconut filled with rum and honey, served with a straw. Behind the beach there are lakes and swamps, so take precautions against mosquitoes and the sandflies that appear in the evening.

However, if you are traveling independently, you can stop at various smaller beaches where sun shades can be rented and there are a couple of beachside grill restaurants along the way, where you can eat lobster and wash it down with a mojito.

TOPES DE COLLANTES

There are lots of day trips offered from Trinidad, including hiking, horse riding, diving, sailing to sandy cays, or more sightseeing, all of which are worthwhile, depending on how much time you've got. To get close to nature, see lots of birds and flowers, enjoy magnificent views, swim in cool mountain pools, and hike on forest trails, a trip to the **Gran Parque Nacional Topes de Collantes** ❻ in the forested Sierra Escambray is recommended. If you have no car then reserve a place on a tour, of which there are many and varied options.

Head west out of Trinidad for just over 3 miles (5 km) on the main road west to Cienfuegos then turn right on the 4-152

Swimming in Topes de Collantes national park

just before Piti Fajardo to head to Topes de Collantes, 13 miles (21 km) from Trinidad. Half way up, stop at the Mirador, 1,968 ft (600 m) above sea level, for stunning views of the city and the peninsula and a drink at the rustic bar.

Topes de Collantes Visitors' Center is at the entrance. Here you pay an entry fee to the National Park, find maps, book tours, and hire guides. Guides are mandatory for any excursion in the National Park. There is a settlement here, also known as Topes de Collantes. Originally inhabited by coffee farmers, in 1954 General Batista ordered the construction of a sanatorium for sufferers of tuberculosis, which was later converted to a hotel, called Kurhotel. He also built a house for his wife here and there are a few smaller hotels. There is a small museum, **Plaza de las Memorias** (Mon–Sat, 8am–5pm), which tells the history of the settlement and its hotels.

On the main approach road from Trinidad, just before the hotels, is the **Museo de Arte Cubano Contemporáneo** (8am–8pm; charge), showcasing artworks previously held in the sanatorium. Formerly the house of a Cuban senator, its galleries contain some 70 works by Cuban masters. Next door is the **Bar-Restaurante Gran Nena** (see ⑨), where you can have lunch and next to that is a lovely orchard of bananas, avocados, oranges, and papayas and you can walk along a path to a cave.

Nearby is the **Casa del Café** (see ⑥), part museum, part café (7am–7pm, 400 yards/m south of Kurhotel), where you can learn about the history of coffee cultivation in the area and taste the local varieties. Just up the road is the **Jardín de Variedades del Café**, a garden with 25 varieties of coffee plants.

TRAILS

The most popular hike is the 1.5-mile (2.5-km), 2.5-hour trek through coffee plantations, past traditional farmers' houses to the **Salto del Caburní**, a 203-ft (62-m) waterfall cascading down a rock wall into a series of swimming pools. The trail starts beside the Villa Caburní and zigzags down to the falls, which can be dry if there's a drought.

Paseo Ecológico is a 0.62-mile (1-km) path from the Kurhotel to the hotel Los Helechos, under a canopy of pines and eucalyptus and bordered by ferns and the *mariposa* or butterfly lily (*Hedychium coronarium*), Cuba's national flower, which blooms with a sweet perfume from June to early September.

From the Casa de Café you can hike the scenic 1.9-mile (3-km) trail **La Batata**, heading west to a cave system with underground river and several levels of natural pools. From this trail you can continue along the Magic Carpet (**Alfombra Mágica**) Trail to **Finca Codina**, an old coffee farm which today

Lush Topes de Collantes

is used by birdwatchers, hikers, and tour parties. There are leaky tents you can camp in but most people prefer to sleep on the veranda in case it rains. It is used mainly as a lunch stop for tour parties, offering a sumptuous meal of roast suckling pig and all the trimmings. You can also indulge in a mud bath, stroll through an orchid garden or follow paths to waterfalls and caves.

Return to Trinidad the same way you arrived.

Food and Drink

① BAR LA ESCALINATA

Half way up the steps leading to the Casa de la Música; bar 9am–2am, live bands 9am–8pm, show 9pm; $

Open-air music venue with a lovely view towards the Plaza Mayor, this is a great place for a sunset cocktail. You can sit at tables but if they are full, find a space on the steps where you can drink your beer or mojito. It is closed if it rains.

② PALENQUE DE LOS CONGOS REALES

Fernando H Echerrí entre La Escalinata y Casa de la Trova; tel: 41-994 512; 10am–midnight, 1am on Sat; $

This is a pleasant, shady place for a drink where you can often hear live bands playing or watch an Afro-Cuban dance show. *Son* and salsa at night.

③ LA CANCHÁNCHARA

Villena 78; 10am-10.45pm; $$

Known for its house cocktail of the same name made of rum, honey, and lime, served in earthenware pots, it is often full with tour parties during the day, but is quieter in the evenings. There is usually live music and food is available.

④ VISTA GOURMET

Callejón de Galdós 28 entre EV Muñoz y Callejón de los Gallegos; tel: 41-996 700; lunch and dinner; $$

This restaurant is on the roof terrace of a colonial house and enjoys a lovely view over the town. There is a buffet for your first course and for dessert, but you order your main course from a menu. Buffets aren't to everyone's taste, but the main courses are usually good and a bit different from the average Cuban menu.

⑤ GRAN NENA

Topes de Collantes; tel: 41-540 338; 10am-9pm; $

This restaurant serves the usual comida criolla, with rather slow service so be prepared to relax and wait.

⑥ CASA DEL CAFÉ

Topes de Collantes, 400 yards/m south of the Kurhotel; 7am–7pm; $

Try local varieties of coffee here and find out about the history of coffee cultivation in the area.

Catching up in Parque Vidal

SANTA CLARA

Famous for being the last resting place of the iconic guerrillero Che Guevara, the youthful university city of Santa Clara is on the main highway heading east from Havana, surrounded by fertile agricultural land, once entirely given over to sugar cane.

DISTANCE: 3 miles (5 km) of walking, 3 miles (5 km) of driving
TIME: One day
START: Parque Vidal, Santa Clara
END: Parque Vidal, Santa Clara
POINTS TO NOTE: Everything in the town center is within walking distance but hire a taxi or *bicitaxi* to get to the Plaza de la Revolución.

Santa Clara was the site of the last and decisive battle of the Revolution when Che Guevara and his guerrilla army defeated General Batista's troops by ambushing the train carrying them east. Although Santa Clara is famous for its Revolutionary associations, it is also known for its artistic and cultural life. A university town with a large student population, it is busy and lively, day and night and there is always something going on.

Santa Clara was founded in 1689 by a group of families from Remedios. They parcelled out the land and became the local oligarchy, building up the set-tlement and their fortunes by growing tobacco and sugar, rearing cattle, and working the Malezas copper mines, as well as trading with both ends of the island. The railroad arrived in 1873, increasing prosperity, and in 1895, when the island was divided into six provinces, Santa Clara became the capital city of the large province of Las Villas.

PARQUE VIDAL

Santa Clara's main square is the delightful, leafy **Parque Vidal ❶**, with a graceful band stand. The municipal band plays at 8pm on Sundays and Thursdays, listened to by appreciative crowds enjoying the evening air. The Parque is a Wi-Fi hotspot and the hub of the city's social life, where the young congregate at weekends, children have music and dance activities, and the older generation dance on Sunday afternoons. There are several places where you can sit and take in the atmosphere.

A monument marks the spot where Independence hero Leoncio Vidal was killed in 1896, and benches line the

One way to get around   *Casa de Cultura Juan Marinello Vidaurreta*

promenades that cross and encircle the park. Until 1894 a fence separated the inner promenade for whites from the outer area for blacks. There is also a bronze statue of Marta Abreu de Estévez, one of the city's benefactors, and another called El Niño de la Bota Infortunada, of a small boy carrying water in his leaky boot. Colonnaded buildings from the late 19th and early 20th centuries line the square, several of which have been or are being renovated.

In the southwest corner of the square is the ugly, green **Hotel Santa Clara Libre**, a tower block built in the Batista era, distinguished by a façade still riddled with shrapnel from the 1958 campaign. Next to the hotel and slightly overshadowed by it is the **Casa de Cultura Juan Marinello Vidaurreta**, now a National Monument for its architectural value. A variety of cultural events are held here, often spilling out into the Parque.

Walk along the west side of the square and on the corner of the north side is another National Monument, the lovely **Teatro La Caridad** (Mon–Sat 9am–4pm; charge, or catch a performance), built in the 1880s. Despite several restorations, it contains more original features than any other theatre in Cuba, including the beautiful frescoes and the stage machinery, with miles of ropes, levers, pulleys and counterweights. It is spectacular and well worth going in. Attached to it is **La Marquesina** (see ❶), a pleasant café/bar you might like to come back to at the end of your day.

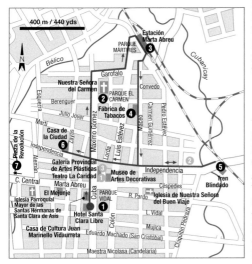

NORTH OF PARQUE VIDAL

Behind the theatre, on Máximo Gómez, is the **Galería Provincial de Artes Plásticas** (Tue–Thu 9am–5pm, Fri–Sat 2–10pm, Sun 6–10pm, free), the largest art gallery outside Havana. Originally a family house built in the 19th century,

The evocative Monumento Che Guevara

it has recently been completely restored to exhibit artworks by national and international artists. There is often live music here too, especially at weekends.

Continue north along Máximo Gómez until you get to **Parque El Carmen ②**. The pretty, white 18th century church of **Nuestra Señora del Carmen** is built on the hill where Santa Clara's founding families held their first Mass. In the park outside there is a 1951 marble monument to the families who founded

Cigar rollers at work

the city: a spiral construction surrounding a tamarind tree.

Head east along Garofalo, the street running along the north side of Parque el Carmen, turn left along Luis Estévez and you come to the **Marta Abreu ③** railway station at Parque Mártires. This is a very impressive station architecturally, a national monument, and recently renovated. The shady park contains a bust of Martí and a monument to martyrs.

Leave the park on Maceo heading south a couple of blocks to reach the **Fábrica de Tabacos ④** (Maceo entre Julio Jover y Berenguer; tel: 42-202 211; guided tours Mon–Fri 9am–1.30pm; charge), the largest cigar factory outside Havana where several brands are made. The short tours are interesting and better than those in Havana because you get closer to the workers. Get a ticket from a tour agency in advance or from the coffee, rum, and cigar shop opposite: La Veguita, and wait your turn in reception.

EAST OF PARQUE VIDAL

Another couple of blocks down Maceo and you come to Independencia. Turn left here, heading east and keep going until you reach the river. Just before the bridge is **Café Museo Revolución** (see ②), exhibiting a fascinating private collection of memorabilia of Fidel and Che, with the advantage of serving you

The attack of the Tren Blindado was a decisive win for Che and his Rebel Army

an optional coffee, cold drink, or snack while you browse.

On your right just after the bridge, you will see the **Tren Blindado** ❺ (Armoured Train; Mon–Sat 8am–5pm). This train, loaded with 408 government soldiers and munitions, was sent from Havana to stop the Rebel Army's advance, but was derailed at a critical moment during the battle for Santa Clara, when it was attacked on December 29, 1958 by 23 rebels under Che Guevara's command with guns and Molotov cocktails. To prevent the men and munitions getting through, Che himself ripped up the lines with a bulldozer, derailing the train and subsequently winning the battle. Both the bulldozer and three of the train's five carriages have been preserved in situ.

Return over the bridge and head west again along Independencia. This is the main commercial street in the city, commonly known as El Bulevar, and much of it is pedestrian-only. A good lunch stop is the blue and white **Santa Rosalía** (see ❸) just off El Bulevar on Máximo Gómez.

WEST OF PARQUE VIDAL

Two blocks further along Independencia on the right hand side is **La Casa de la Ciudad** ❻ (Independencia esq Zayas; tel: 42-205 593; 8am–5pm and for evening events). Dating from 1860, the building was formerly a grand residence but it is now a progressive cultural center, with art exhibitions, workshops, and a film museum. Dance nights and live music events are held in the courtyard. It is a fine example of colonial domestic architecture, with huge doors and windows covered with ornate *rejas*, or grills, some lovely stained glass and decorative paintwork.

PLAZA DE LA REVOLUCIÓN ERNESTO GUEVARA

The plaza, on the far west side of town, is best reached by *bicitaxi*, having first agreed a price. The **Plaza de la Revolución Ernesto Guevara** ❼, is the usual place for revolutionary gatherings. It is dominated by one of Cuba's finest revolutionary statues, the **Monumento Che Guevara**, a giant bronze figure of Che, shown carrying a machine gun with his other arm in a sling – he broke it when he fell from a building during the battle for Santa Clara in 1958 – bearing the legend 'Hasta la Victoria Siempre' (ever onward to victory). It stands above a bas-relief scene of his battles and an inscription of the letter Che wrote to Fidel when he left Cuba to continue the struggle abroad. It was designed by José Delarra (1938–2003), an avid admirer of the Argentine rebel, who created a further 14 sculptures depicting scenes of the exploits of Che and his guerrilleros in the province of Villa Clara.

Beneath Che's statue is the **Mausoleo** (Tue–Sun 9am–5pm; no cameras, free), where the remains of Che and 29

Parque Vidal is the hub of social life in Santa Clara

of his co-revolutionaries were interred in 1997, after being recovered from Bolivia. The mausoleum, with its low ceiling and construction almost entirely of stone, has the look and feel of a cave. An eternal flame was lit by Fidel Castro. Few visitors fail to be moved by the aura of reverence.

Beside the mausoleum there is also an interesting museum, the **Museo Histórico de la Revolución** (Tue–Sun 9am–5pm; free), featuring revolutionary memorabilia and some great photographs. There is also sometimes a video about Che and his role in the Revolution. Behind the complex there is a beautifully landscaped cemetery designed for all the men and women who fought under Che's command.

Return to the town centre in time to enjoy a sunset drink in Parque Vidal and a night on the town. The **Museo de Artes Decorativas** (Marta Abreu esq Luís Estévez; Mon–Thu 9am–6pm, Fri–Sat 9am–10pm, Sun 9am–noon, 6–10pm; charge) is on the north side of the Parque, if you have the energy. Built as a family home in the 18th century in typical Spanish colonial style with rooms around a central courtyard, it exhibits furniture and homeware from the 18th, 19th and 20th centuries. Alternatively, find a seat in **La Marquesina** and watch the world go by.

Food and Drink

① LA MARQUESINA
Teatro La Caridad, Máximo Gómez esq Marta Abreu; $
A pleasant place to stop during the day for a coffee or cold drink and a snack, while at night it is a popular watering hole for all ages, with live music until midnight.

② CAFÉ MUSEO REVOLUCIÓN
Independencia 313, Santa Clara, just over the bridge from El Tren Blindado; tel: 42-216 145; 11am–11pm; $
Part museum, part café, with an intriguing private collection of revolutionary memorabilia amassed over many years by the family running the snack bar. Staff are helpful and some speak English, so they can explain what you are seeing while they serve you coffee, tea, a cold drink, beer or cocktail, with or without alcohol. Sandwiches are available.

③ SANTA ROSALÍA
Máximo Gómez 2 entre Marta Abreu y Independencia (Bulevar); tel: 42-201 438; 11am–11pm, bar until 2am; $$
Lovely old colonial building with a central patio for indoor or outdoor dining. This is a state restaurant and often used by tour parties, when a buffet is laid on, but à la carte is also available. The food is usually good and the service is all right. At weekends it is a popular music and dance venue at night.

Sleepy Remedios

REMEDIOS AND THE CAYS

The 500-year old town of Remedios, known for its Christmas festivities, is within striking distance of the impressive beaches of the cays off the north coast. While it may not be as picturesque as Trinidad, Remedios scores top marks for its tranquility and relative lack of tourists.

DISTANCE: 3 miles (5 km) of walking, 63 miles (100 km) driving
TIME: One day
START: Remedios
END: Cayo Santa María
POINTS TO NOTE: Spend the morning looking round Remedios and the afternoon on the beach. Public transport is limited so it is easier to hire a car or taxi. Car hire companies are all outside Santa Clara at the airport. A return trip to the beach is feasible, or you might want to spend the night on the cays, in which case you will need to book a hotel in advance. Take swimsuit, sun protection and water to the beach, which is very exposed. The only ATM on the cays is next to the Medical Centre on Cayo Santa María.

REMEDIOS

Some 30 miles (45 km) northeast of Santa Clara (heading toward the north coast) is **San Juan de Remedios**, a sleepy, engaging little colonial town and the oldest settlement in the province of Villa Clara. Founded by Vasco Porcallo de Figueroa in 1513–15 as probably the third of eight *villas*, it was moved in 1544 and in 1578 and never achieved the status of the other *villas*. A fire in 1692 meant that all the colonial buildings were built after that date. There has been very little recent urban development here, something the town has in common with Trinidad.

In 2015, the government marked the 500th anniversary of the town's foundation by investing in renovation works, new hotels, road surfacing, Wi-Fi and other projects. It still retains its slow pace of life, however, and all traffic moves at the pace of the many bicycles and *bicitaxis*.

PLAZA MARTÍ

Plaza Martí, the town's pleasantly spacious central square, has a charming bandstand and Remedios is the only town in Cuba to possess two churches on its main plaza. The most stunning edifice in Remedios is the **Iglesia Parroquia Mayor de San Juan**

Iglesia de Nuestra Señora del Buen Viaje

Bautista de Remedios ❶ (Mon–Fri 9am–noon, 2–5pm, or during Mass at other times, or seek out the church warden at the rear), bordering the east side of Plaza Martí. The old church, built in 1692 on the foundations of an earlier one, was severely damaged by a 1939 earthquake, but a millionaire penitent underwrote a 10-year renovation, discovering a gold painted altar and carved beams under layers of encrusted paint and false ceilings. The gilded altar is seen in its full glory when the lights are turned on.

On the west side of the Plaza, on Máximo Gómez, is the long-established (possibly the oldest restaurant in Cuba) **Bar El Louvre** (see ❶), a pleasant place for a drink or snack sitting watching the world go by.

The second church, the simpler **Iglesia de Nuestra Señora del Buen Viaje** ❷, tucked in the northeast corner of the Plaza, is currently under renovation. Legend has it that in 1600, some fishermen discovered a wooden box in the mangroves which contained the image carved in wood of the Virgin Mary with the child Jesus in her arms. It had come from Barcelona, Spain, and was relatively unscathed by the journey. The church is built on the spot where they brought the Virgin, surrounding her with flowers and candles on a makeshift altar.

On the east side of the Plaza is the **Museo de la Música Alejandro García Caturla** ❸ (Mon–Sat 9am–noon, 1–5pm), originally the home of Alejandro García Caturla, a lawyer who devoted his live to music and became one of Cuba's most famous avant-garde composers. Caturla broke with the conventions of his class in every way, marrying a black woman and fighting corruption. In 1940, at the age of 34, he was murdered by a policeman he was about to sentence for beating up a prostitute. The museum exhibits his personal effects, scores, musical instruments and documents relating to his work. There are

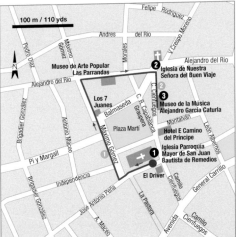

Alejandro García museum

Parrandas fireworks

also art exhibitions and information on other musicians from the area.

It is best to eat in Remedios before setting off for the cays as there are few options out there. On the same side of the Plaza as the Museo de la Música is **Portales a la Plaza** (see ❷), where you can eat a typical Cuban meal and pay local prices. There are other restaurants serving better food but here you won't be swamped by tour parties.

CAYOS DE LA HERRADURA

The cays off the north coast are collectively known as the **Cayos de la Herradura** and for many years they were

Herons in Cayo Santa María

left undeveloped as Fidel Castro liked to fish here as a young man. Now, however, all-inclusive resorts have been

Festivals

Remedios is famous for its *parrandas*, when groups advance through the streets to rouse people for the pre-dawn Mass held to honor San Juan de los Remedios on December 24. The fascinating and unmissable **Museo de Arte Popular Las Parrandas** (Alejandro del Río 74 entre Enrique Malaret y Máximo Gómez; Tue–Sat 9am–noon, 1–6pm, Sun 9am–1pm; extra charge for guide and photos) displays instruments heard during the celebrations, and many of the costumes and floats. Neighboring districts (Carmen, identified by a sparrow-hawk and a globe, and San Salvador, whose symbol is a rooster) spend the week between Christmas Eve and New Year's Eve competing for the best *carroza* (parade float). For months beforehand, artists and engineers secretly plan and build a so-called *trabajo de plaza*, a great tower of light that represents their neighborhood; it can reach up to 90 ft (28 m). The *parrandas* start when darkness falls, with the unveiling of these incredible confections, and continue until dawn, with musicians playing traditional polkas. Paraders carry handmade lanterns and banners, there are tableaux on dazzling floats, and fireworks as thrilling as they are menacing.

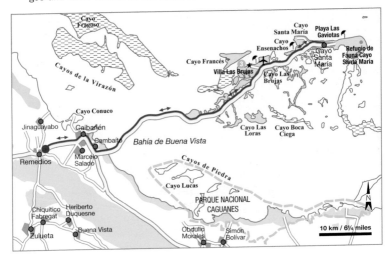

and are being built, aided by the construction of a 30-mile (48-km) causeway from just east of Caibarién to three of the cays. The main road bypasses the centre of Caibarién, a rather run down fishing port, by turning right at the statue of a huge crab on the edge of town and then right again at the next junction. The road to the causeway is well signed at a road bridge where you take the slip road on the right to go over it and effectively turn left. Passports are checked at the toll booth (*peaje*) where you pay CUC$2 per car.

The road strikes out across the flat water of the lagoons and mangroves surrounding the cays, with numbered bridges. Look out for flocks of flamingos and other waders in the shallows.

At Bridge 36 you reach **Cayo Las Brujas**, where there is an airstrip, a marina and the small hotel, **Villa Las Brujas**, the first to be built on the cays. Perched up on rocks overlooking the beach, it is a pleasant place to stop for a drink or meal (see ③), even if you don't stay there. It is the only non-resort hotel here.

The road continues to **Cayo Ensenachos** and on to **Cayo Santa María**, the largest cay where most of the resorts have been built along the beach. A small replica village in colonial style, called **El Pueblo**, has souvenir shops and a café, but there are no restaurants other than in the hotels.

At the end of the paved road, follow the dirt track a short way to a parking area in the trees. This is a protected

Idyllic Cayo Ensenachos

area and you have to pay the park guards an entry fee. Follow the trail through the dry tropical forest, looking out for lizards, birds, and other creatures, until you come over dunes to the spectacular **Playa Las Gaviotas**, an extensive, open, undeveloped beach at the end of the hotel strip. Here there are no bars, no sunbeds, no shade, and very few people. The sand is soft and white and the sea is a range of turquoise hues where it is shallow, until it becomes a deep blue further out. It is the perfect place to relax at the end of a long day, strolling in the warm shallows spotting herons fishing.

Getting ready to sail, Cayo Santa María

Food and Drink

🅿 BAR EL LOUVRE

Máximo Gómez 122; $

Sit in the shade or the sunshine overlooking the square and watch the world go by with a coffee, beer, cocktail, or snack. Food is limited to sandwiches, pasta or pizza, but it is cheap and filling. Pleasant place for a sunset daiquiri before dinner.

🅿 PORTALES A LA PLAZA

Plaza Martí, entre Alejandro del Río y Montalván; lunch and dinner from 6.30pm; $

Very simple set menu but popular with Cuban families as well as visitors. The food is cooked well and the service is friendly, but they do run out of things. There may be no beer or no bottled water, no dessert, no coffee, but go with the flow and you'll enjoy what they do have. The state-owned restaurant is in a lovely colonial house, cool and smart.

🅿 EL FARALLON, VILLA LAS BRUJAS

Cayo Las Brujas; tel: 42-350 199; www.gaviota-grupo.com; $$

This restaurant at the only non-resort hotel on the cays is perched on rocks and has a lovely view down to the 1.2-mile (2-km) beach with seating indoors or outdoors. The menu is limited and the service is mostly slow, but the food is adequate.

The brightly colored Plaza San Juan de Dios

CAMAGÜEY WALKING TOUR

Camagüey is a place of beauty, culture, and tradition. The old town is a delight: narrow, twisting streets wind from the river, lined by rows of small, rainbow-colored, stuccoed houses, with lush courtyards that can be glimpsed through ancient wooden doors. However, don't come expecting another Trinidad: Camagüey is quite different.

DISTANCE: 6 miles (10 km) of walking
TIME: One day
START: Parque Ignacio Agramonte, Camagüey
END: Museo Provincial Ignacio Agramonte, Camagüey
POINTS TO NOTE: The city can be tricky to find your way around, partly because of the irregular street layout but also because several streets have two names. If you get tired of walking, hire a *bicitaxi*, which will give you some shade too.

The city of Camagüey is a cultural oasis in an otherwise arid province, where cows seem to outnumber people. Its cattle pastures support both dairy and beef cattle and vaqueros (cowboys) wearing broad-brimmed hats and dangling machetes, can be seen herding stock from astride their horses, lassos flying.

The city is one of Diego Velázquez' seven original settlements, founded as the Villa of Santa María del Puerto Príncipe in 1514. It was twice moved, razed

by Henry Morgan's crew in 1668 then rebuilt soon after, with a street plan that seems designed to help ambush future invaders. Declared a Unesco World Heritage Site in 2008, it is full of architectural gems and has a rich artistic tradition.

PARQUE IGNACIO AGRAMONTE

Camagüey has spawned a number of eminent men, several of whom have achieved international fame. Ignacio Agramonte is the great warrior who battled for five years against the colonial Spanish but never lived to see independence (the inhabitants of Camagüey are called *agromonteros* in his honor). **Parque Ignacio Agramonte ❶** is the nearest thing Camagüey has to a main square. The dramatic mounted figure of Agramonte is the centerpiece.

On the south side, the 19th-century **Catedral** is worth a peek. Its wooden ceiling is its best feature. If you ask, you may be allowed to climb spiral steps to the bell tower for a wonderful view (donation appreciated). On the west side is the Casa de la Trova Patricio Bal-

Artist's studio

lagas Palacios, where you can hear traditional music in the courtyard at any time, day or night. At the entrance is a shop where you can buy music.

A block west of the Parque, Carlos J. Finlay's birthplace at Cristo 5 between Lugareño and Callejón del Templador (tel: 32-296-745) is open to the public. He was born in 1833 to a family of mixed French and Scottish origins and later pursued his scientific studies in Paris and Philadelphia. His discovery in 1881 that the Aedes mosquito was the vector for yellow fever affected the world's health. By controlling the mosquito population, the spread of both yellow fever and malaria were checked, a factor of particular importance in the construction of the Panama Canal. Finlay became the chief health officer in Cuba at the beginning of the 20th century and died in Havana in 1915.

PLAZA DEL CARMEN

The old church of **Nuestra Señora del Carmen** lies several blocks west of the square along Calle Martí, on the beautifully restored **Plaza del Carmen ❷**. The old hospital alongside the church is now the offices of the Historiador de la Ciudad, where all the restoration works are planned. The plaza is dotted with *tinajones* as well as sculptures by Martha Jiménez Pérez (her gallery is on the plaza) of gossiping women, a courting couple, and a man reading a newspaper. The real-life models can often be seen

alongside their statues. The *tinajones* are a prominent feature in Camagüey – round, wide-mouthed earthenware jugs, modeled on the big-bellied jars that came from Spain filled with wines and oils. Cuban versions were created by local potters to solve a pressing problem: Camagüey had almost no water sources, and rainfall, while abundant, was seasonal. You still see *tinajones* in the shady courtyard of many Camagüeyan households, and water sellers still ply the streets. Ranging in size from large to enormous, some of the *tinajones* still in use were made more than a century ago.

There are restaurants here, such as **El Paso** (see ❶), where you can sit and

A lovely restaurant courtyard

Jiménez Pérez sculpture on Plaza del Carmen

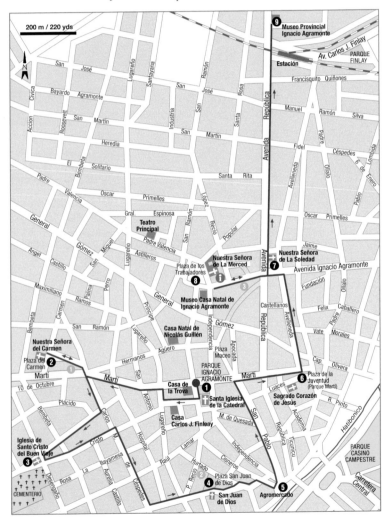

Fruit sold here   *Browsing at the Agromercado*

have a drink, or take a break on one of the benches and watch the world go by.

While in this area, walk a few blocks south to the **Iglesia de Santo Cristo del Buen Viaje ❸**. The interest here lies mainly in the adjacent **cemetery**, one of the finest in the country, much frequented by local people who like to stroll around, as well as visiting family graves. Running eastward, back toward the center, Calle Cristo has road-side flower-sellers, and a couple of local bars.

PLAZA SAN JUAN DE DIOS

Rivaling the Plaza del Carmen for the honor of being the loveliest place in Camagüey is the restored, 18th-century **Plaza San Juan de Dios ❹**, south of Parque Agramonte. Now a national monument, the square is peaceful and surrounded by brightly colored houses with elegant wooden *rejas* (grilles), and tall doors and windows. The plaza is dominated by the **Iglesia San Juan de Dios**, a small, intimate church with a fine mahogany ceiling and altar.

Adjacent, the old hospital, the first ever built in town, was where the body of Agramonte was brought before his interment in the cemetery. Now the hospital is the local heritage office, Centro Provincial de Patrimonio Cultural.

Two of the finest buildings on the plaza are restaurants, **La Campana de Toledo** and the **Parador de los Tres Reyes**, popular with day-trippers. Another is **1800** (see ❼), with tables out on the square,

a good place to stop for refreshment and to watch the world go by.

THE RIVERSIDE

A couple of blocks east of Plaza San Juan de Dios, the **Agromercado ❺** (farmers' market), on the banks of the river, is a great place to appreciate the *agramonteros'* renowned love of good food. In addition to stands selling fresh produce are simple kitchens serving hot meals. It's a lively spot, shaded by palms and tropical foliage, and with vendors noisily hawking their produce: piles of glossy mangos, tomatoes, and peppers, strings of garlic, and heaps of mamey. On the eastern bank of the Hatibonico River, Parque Casino Campestre was used in colonial times for cattle shows, fairs, dances, and other social activities.

Freshly squeezed guarapo, sugar cane juice

Plaza de los Trabajadores

PLAZA DE LA JUVENTUD

Heading north up Calle San Pablo and turning right on Calle Martí you come to the **Plaza de la Juventud** ❻, to give it the official name, but local people know it as **Parque Martí**. This quiet square is dominated by the **Sagrado Corazón de Jesús**, an imposing neo-Gothic church built in 1920. Its stained glass windows were damaged during the Revolution and restoration started only in 2001. Completed in 2013 with a new roof and other works, the whole square has also been given a facelift and repainted.

Che mural, Plaza de los Trabajadores

PLAZA DE LOS TRABAJADORES

From Parque Martí walk north along Avellaneda until you get to the 18th-century **Nuestra Señora de la Soledad** ❼ on Plaza de la Soledad. Its red-brick exterior looks unpromising, but inside you are greeted by glorious decoration on the arches and pillars, topped by a splendid vaulted ceiling. It is a short walk from here along Avenida Ignacio Agramonte to the **Plaza de los Trabajadores** ❽. Just before the Plaza, at Callejón de los Milagros, is an area devoted to cinema, where there are several movie houses and themed cafés and galleries. A restaurant worth trying is **La Isabela** (see ❶), named after a local actor.

The city's most famous son, Ignacio Agramonte (1841–73), was the fighting general of Camagüey's rebel forces during the first War of Independence (he died in action in 1873). The **Museo Casa Natal de Ignacio Agramonte** (Avenida Agramonte, 459, Plaza de los Trabajadores; tel: 32-297-116; Tue–Sat 9am–7pm, Sun 8.30–11.30am; charge) is a museum in the hero's birthplace – a lovely 18th-century mansion, sumptuously furnished with period pieces.

Nuestra Señora de La Merced (opening hours vary), across from Agramonte's birthplace on the **Plaza de los Trabajadores was c**onsidered one of the most splendid churches in the country when it was first built in 1747

View over the city from the Gran Hotel

and is now a National Monument. La Merced has benefitted from (ongoing) restoration: the 20th-century decorated ceiling is particularly striking. The ghoulish may go down the steps beside the altar to see the catacombs.

North of here sits the splendid **Teatro Principal**, which draws the biggest audiences when the Ballet de Camagüey or the local symphony orchestra perform.

NORTH OF THE CENTER

Retrace your steps to Plaza de la Soledad, from where you can walk north along Avenida República, which is pedestrianized until just after the railway line (when it becomes Avenida de los Mártires) where you find the **Museo Provincial Ignacio Agramonte** ❾ (Avenida de los Mártires 2; tel: 32-282-425; Tue–Thu and Sat 10am–6pm, Fri noon–8pm, Sun 10am–2pm; charge), with an eclectic collection ranging from stuffed animals to archaeological finds. It is best known, though, for its fine-art collection. A cavalry barracks in the mid-19th century, the building was converted into a hotel in the first half of the 20th century but became a museum in 1955.

Food and Drink

❶ EL PASO

Hermanos Agüero 261, Plaza del Carmen; tel: 5239 0939; 9am–11pm; $$

A lovely spot at the entrance to the plaza serving traditional Cuban food with seating indoors or outdoors on the plaza or upstairs. Lunch times can be very busy with tour parties but service is efficient and friendly. Happy hour specials if you are here later on for drinks.

❷ RESTAURANTE 1800

Plaza San Juan de Dios; tel: 32-283 619; 9am–1am; $$$

This upmarket *paladar* boasts a most impressive bar of varnished wood and all the furnishings are high quality and elegant. There is seating out on the plaza, or indoors in the dining room, while there is also an inner courtyard where a buffet is laid out. You can eat from the buffet or à la carte, or a combination of the two. The food is good and there is a whole wine cellar to go with it.

❸ LA ISABELA

Ignacio Agramonte, near Plaza de los Trabajadores; T32-221 540; 11am–4pm, 6.30–10pm; $$

Decorated with a cinema theme, movie posters and film reels on the walls, while you sit on director's chairs with famous directors' names on the back. Pasta and thin-crust pizza make a change from rice and beans and the air conditioning is a welcome relief. Service is good and friendly.

Into the Sierra Maestra

HIKING IN THE SIERRA MAESTRA

High in the mountains, away from prying eyes, lies the command post from where Fidel Castro directed the rebel war from the end of 1956. Today, tourists hike the muddy trails to soak up the atmosphere of those times of deprivation and danger.

DISTANCE: 4 or 23 miles (6 or 36 km) of walking, 88 miles (140 km) driving
TIME: One or two days
START: Bayamo
END: Bayamo
POINTS TO NOTE: Wear good hiking footwear and expect to get dirty. The paths get muddy after rain and scrambling up slippery slopes makes you sweaty and filthy. Take plenty of water and snacks. If you are staying overnight on the mountain, warm clothes and a light sleeping bag are recommended as it can be cold, wet and windy. Tip your guide and donate any excess gear at the end of your trip.

The Parque Nacional Turquino covers a large area of humid montane forest in the Sierra Maestra, including Cuba's highest mountain, the Pico Turquino (6,476 ft/1,974 m). There are several endemic plants and animals in the protected area and birdwatching is rewarding. It is particularly exciting to see the trogon, Cuba's national bird, living in Castro's camp.

While most visitors hike the shorter route to the Comandancia de la Plata, there are miles of other trails for the active to explore with a guide. A regular route is up Pico Turquino, staying overnight in a mountain lodge, and these two walks can be combined. If you are fit, this will be a highlight of your trip to Cuba.

SANTO DOMINGO

It is possible to stay at Santo Domingo, but most people come from Bayamo, a drive of about 1 hour 15 minutes, where there is greater availability of accommodations, food, and transportation. Arrange a return trip with a taxi if you don't have a rental car, or book a place on a tour from the city with an agency. Take the road from Bayamo to Manzanillo for 28.5 miles (46 km) and turn off at Yara to Bartolomé Masó, 8.7 miles (14 km) further on. The mountain road starts here, with many steep climbs, via Providencia to Santo Domingo.

During the Revolution, **Santo Domingo ❶** was a rebel camp with a mess hall and workshops. Today these have

The dense Parque Nacional Turquino

been adapted for feeding and entertaining campers. Cabins are partially hidden in the forest by the Yara River. There is a rustic hotel, **Villa Santo Domingo**, and three *casas particulares* in the village, but not much else. The National Parks office is on the left beyond the hotel. All tours start from here and you must get here early to book a place as all tours to the Comandancia de la Plata leave at 8.30–9am. An entry fee and guides are mandatory. If you want to do the two-day hike to Pico Turquino, this must be booked in advance, as numbers are limited on the mountain.

From the National Parks office you are taken by 4WD 3 miles (5 km) up the steepest road in Cuba with a 40-degree gradient, to the parking lot at Alto de Naranjo (3,116 ft/950 m). The trail to the right goes to the Comandancia de la Plata, while the trail to the left heads up Pico Turquino.

LA COMANDANCIA DE LA PLATA

The 2-mile (3-km) trail to **La Comandancia de la Plata ❷** goes up and down hill and parts of it are steep. Halfway there you come to the house of the Medina family, who were the first in the area to help the revolutionaries. Their little family farm looks much the same today, with pigs and chickens roaming around and coffee beans drying on the ground.

At the command station there is a small museum, Castro's bedroom and kitchen (including the bullet-ridden fridge carried up the mountain under fire from Batista's forces), the old hospital and the Radio Rebelde broadcasting station on the highest point, all small wooden buildings spread out over the hillside. Quiet, beautiful and very atmospheric, you get a good idea of how tough life must have been.

The speed of the hike depends on the ability of those in your group, but it

La Comandancia de la Plata, Fidel Castro's former headquarters in the Sierra Maestra

usually takes 3–4 hours. A snack lunch is provided, but you may need another in Santo Domingo at the **Mirador de Arcadia** (see ●) on your return.

PICO TURQUINO

Hikes up Cuba's highest mountain, **Pico Turquino** ❸, are exciting and beautiful. Between out-croppings of mineral and sedimentary rocks, deep green conifers stand alongside precious cedar, mahogany, and trumpet-wood trees. The slopes are dotted with delicate wild orchids and graceful ferns. Although it can be cold and windy, the temperature rarely drops to freezing and there is never any snow. You can't see anything from the summit of Turquino (where there is a bronze bust of José Martí) because of trees, but the views from just before you reach it are magnificent.

From Alto de Naranjo you walk 8 miles (13 km) – 4 to 5 hours – to reach the Aguado de Joaquín mountain lodge where you will sleep overnight. Facili-

ties are basic, but there are bunkbeds with mattresses. You can either hike the remaining 3 miles (5 km) (6 miles/10km round trip) to the summit in the afternoon or the following morning. However, if you want to combine Turquino with a visit to Comandancia de la Plata, you will need to reach the summit the first day, allowing time for the 8-mile (13-km) descent and the 3.7-mile (6-km) hike the second day.

Another option for the second day is to hike down to Las Cuevas on the south coast, although this can be very hard on the knees. This must be arranged in advance because there is no transportation or accommodations in Las Cuevas and no National Parks office, so you will need to be met and picked up there.

Castro training his guerilleros at the camp

Food and Drink

● MIRADOR DE ARCADIA
Near Villa Santo Domingo; tel: 5858 0202; $$
Arcadia and Ernesto run a *casa particular* with a restaurant attached, on a large terrace with several tables and good food, very welcome after a long hike.

The streets of Santiago

SANTIAGO DE CUBA AND THE CASTILLO DEL MORRO

Cuba's second city has a heroic revolutionary past but it is also known for its rich musical traditions and its vigorous carnival. Nestled at the foot of the Sierra Maestra around a bay, Santiago de Cuba is the island's most exotic and ethnically diverse city.

DISTANCE: 3 miles (5 km) of walking, 10 miles (16 km) of driving
TIME: A full day
START: Parque Histórico Abel Santamaría
END: Parque Alameda
POINTS TO NOTE: Streets in the center have two or more names, which can be confusing. Take precautions against the sun; the city is hot and the cemetery is blindingly white with no shade.

Multicultural Santiago de Cuba is where many Haitians, both of white French ancestry, and of black African descent, settled after fleeing the slave uprisings in their country at the end of the 18th century, bringing with them the cachet of the Afro-French culture to blend with that of Afro-Hispanic Cuba. Isolated and remote, the city developed on its own path and is noticeably different from Havana.

The city was badly damaged by Hurricane Sandy in 2012, losing most of its trees as well as many buildings, but subsequent repairs and a facelift to cel-ebrate its 500th anniversary in 2015 mean the center is now smart and attractive again. There is some beautiful colonial architecture – you'll see plenty of graceful hanging balconies, gingerbread latticework, and wrought-iron gates throughout the city.

PARQUE HISTÓRICO ABEL SANTAMARÍA

The **Parque Histórico Abel Santamaría ❶** is a well-used spot, where plants struggle to survive, boys play baseball, and groups of elderly people take exercise classes. The impressive monument in the park is dedicated to Abel Santamaría, Fidel Castro's second-in-command in the 1953 uprising and attack on the Moncada Barracks. It was Santamaría's job to create diversionary fire at the hospital, which he continued to do, unaware that the main assault had failed, until he was surrounded. The rebels were caught and tortured, and most were executed. Batista's men gouged out Santamaría's eyes and presented them to his sister, Haydée, a fellow revo-

Ceramics at the Museo de Ambiente Histórico Cubano

lutionary, to make her talk, but she kept silent. Eye hospitals in Cuba now bear Abel Santamaría's name.

On the other side of Ave de los Libertadores is the site of the main attack, the **Antiguo Cuartel Moncada**, now half elementary school, half museum, the **Museo Histórico 26 de Julio** (Moncada Barracks; entrance on Avenida Moncada; tel: 22-620 157; Tue–Sat 9am–8pm, Sun 9am–1pm), dedicated to the Moncada assault and also the later Revolution. Batista had the bullet holes filled in, but these have now been reconstructed for effect. Inside are revolutionary memorabilia, guns, grenades, documents, photographs, Castro's khaki uniforms, and Che Guevara's muddy boots. The museum is visually strong, and there are multilingual guides.

PLAZA DE DOLORES

Walk south down Avenida de los Libertadores to reach Avenida Victoriano Garzón and turn right to head to the old heart of town. You will soon reach the **Plaza de Marte**, a noisy square where taxis gather, and goat-pulled carts take children for rides on weekend. Turn left down the west side of the square and the right along the busy, commercial

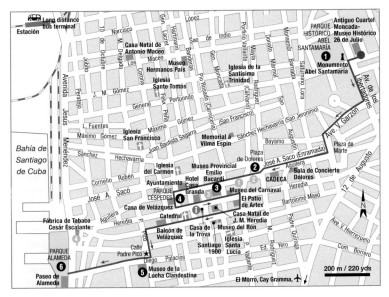

The Ayuntamiento, a landmark of the Revolution

Calle Aguilera to **Plaza de Dolores ❷**, a pleasant open space, more a widening of the street than a square, known as Bulevar. There are several restaurants here including **Isabelica** (see ❶), a café known for its variety of coffees, or **Café Constantin** (see ❷), if you fancy ice cream or a snack with your coffee. In a former church, Nuestra Señora de Dolores, the **Sala de Concierto Dolores** (Aguilera entre Reloj y Clarín) is known for its recitals of choral and orchestral music and has excellent acoustics.

Continuing west down Calle Aguilera, you come to the **Museo Provincial Emilio Bacardí ❸** (entrance on Pío Rosado; tel: 22-628 402; Mon noon–9pm, Tue–Sat 9am–9pm, Sun 9am–1pm; guided tour in English), Santiago's most interesting museum. It was founded in 1899 by Emilio Bacardí Moreau, a Cuban writer and the first mayor of Santiago, although he is more famous for his Caney Rum distillery, which was moved to Puerto Rico after the Revolution to produce the re-named and globally popular Bacardi Rum.

The museum contains some first-rate Cuban art (including works by the talented José Joaquín Tejada Revilla), some colonial European paintings and memorabilia from Cuba's wars of independence, historic documents, flags, maps, and weapons. There is also an archaeology section with indigenous artifacts, an Egyptian mummy – bought by Emilio Bacardí, a keen collector, on a visit to Egypt in 1912 – several skeletons from Paracas in Peru, and a shrunken head.

PARQUE CÉSPEDES

Continue west along Aguilera until you get to the very center of the city at **Parque Céspedes ❹**. The colonial square has a bust of Carlos Manuel de Céspedes in the middle and many of the city's most venerable buildings surround it. Here you will find young and old gathering to exchange news or simply watch the world go by. It is also a place where visitors are likely to get a lot of requests for money or gifts from the persistent *jineteros* (hustlers) of both sexes who congregate here.

The first building you come to on y our right is a splendid neo-colonial white building with blue shutters. This is the **Ayuntamiento** (town hall), from the balcony of which Castro announced the triumph of the Revolution on January 2, 1959.

Continue round in an anti-clockwise direction and you come to Cuba's oldest house in the northwest corner, distinguished by its black-slatted balconies. The **Casa de Velázquez** houses the **Museo de Ambiente Histórico Cubano** (tel: 22-652 652; Sat–Thu 9am–5pm, Fri 2–5pm; multilingual guided tour, camera fee). A solid-stone structure with Moorish-style screened balconies, glorious cedar ceilings (*alfarjes*), floor-to-ceiling shutters, and two lovely courtyards, the house was built between 1516 and

Catedral de Nuestra Señora de la Asunción

1530 and is said to be the oldest home in Cuba. In the 16th century, Governor Diego Velázquez used the first floor as his office and the upper floor as his residence. Among its collection are European tapestries, crystal, paintings, ceramics, and other antiques. *Peñas* (musical performances) are sometimes held here and you may hear musicians practicing in the courtyard.

Dominating the park on the south side is the **Catedral de Nuestra Señora de la Asunción** (Tue–Sat 8am–noon, 5–7.30pm, Sun 8–11am, 5–6.30pm; free), a vast basilica rebuilt four times since the first one was completed in 1524, because of earthquakes or pirate attacks. The current building dates from 1818, with further restoration and decoration added in the 20th century. There is a painted wooden altar and hand-carved choir stalls.

On the east side of the square is the elegant **Hotel Casa Granda**. The hotel was once a high-society spot where the Cuban elite gathered on the rooftop terrace to sip rum, dance, and smoke cigars. Anyone who was anyone could be seen here and famous patrons included many famous movie stars, singers and sports champions, including baseball legend Babe Ruth. However, during the 1950s it teemed with US spies and Cuban rebels. One of the hotel's former guests was the author, Graham Greene, who came here to interview Castro (the interview never took place) and used the setting for a scene in his book *Our Man in Havana*. The hotel has been restored but still has an air of faded grandeur. Having a drink on the roof terrace at sunset is still delightful, while a drink, snack, or lunch at the ground-floor café is a good way of watching the square without being hassled.

CALLE HEREDIA

Having walked round three sides of the square, exit Parque Céspedes heading east along Calle Heredia, which is known for its music. Close to the **Casa Granda** is the **Casa de la Trova** (Heredia 208; tel: 22-652 689), the most famous of Cuba's music venues where all the Cuban greats have performed. All week long, local musicians perform acts that range from somber Spanish guitar classics to vibrant Afro-Cuban drumming; from solo acts to 12-piece bands, trained professionals to talented amateurs. Opposite the Casa de la Trova is a nice place for lunch, **El Holandés** (see ③), where you can sit on the balcony overlooking the street.

Further along the street on the left is the **Museo del Carnaval** (Heredia esq Carnicería; tel: 22-626 955, Tue-Sun 9am-6pm) where there are some great costumes and *cabezudos* (big-headed carnival figures) and faded photographs depicting carnival's history. In the courtyard you can watch Afro-Cuban music and dance sessions daily (except Saturday) at 4pm.

Casa de la Trova memorabilia   *Live music at El Patio de Artex*

Nearly opposite, the **Casa Natal de José María Heredia** (Tue–Sun 9am–6pm) is the birthplace of José María Heredia (1803–39), one of the first Cuban poets to champion national independence. It's a peaceful, attractive house dedicated to his life with original furnishings and occasional poetry workshops held in the courtyard.

On the same side as the Carnival Museum, is **El Patio de Artex** (Heredia 304 entre Carnicería y Calvario; tel: 22-654 814), a friendly place to hear great live music with lots of dancing. It is the former home of artists Félix and José Joaquín Tejada Revilla. There is often music and dancing at 11am and you can hear son at 5pm daily, while in the evenings and late into the night live bands play. There is a bar for drinks and handicrafts for sale.

Double back by heading south down Calvario and then west along Bartolomé Masó (San Basilio) to visit the **Museo del Ron** (San Basilio 358 esq Carnicería, tel: 22-623 737; Mon–Sat 9am–5pm; charge includes a tot of rum). There are some interesting exhibits in this pretty colonial house around a central courtyard, but it is not as extensive as the equivalent museum in Havana.

PADRE PICO

At Calle Padre Pico you come to one of the prettiest streets in the city, featuring steps on the hillside. This is the Tivolí district, where French refugees fleeing the slave rebellion in Haiti built their houses. When Emilio Bacardí was mayor, he had the street and its steps renovated and named them after Bernardo del Pico, a priest who had helped the poor. Castro used their strategic location to fire on Batista's forces during the Revolution and certainly they offer commanding views of the bay and mountains around Santiago.

Turn south and at the corner of Padre Pico and Diego Palacios (Santa Rita) turn right. On the next corner is the yellow **Museo de la Lucha Clandestina** ❺ (Museum of the Underground Struggle; Gen Jesús Rabi 1 esq Diego Palacios; tel: 22-624 689; Tue–Sun 9am–5pm) in a beautifully restored colonial mansion with fine views. It is dedicated to the heroes of the 26th of July Movement, particularly Frank País, and highlights the help that local people gave to the revolutionaries from 1953 onwards. In 1956 guerrillas fire-bombed the Batista police station here, to divert attention from the Granma landing along the coast, which brought the Castros and Che Guevara to the island to start the Revolution.

PARQUE ALAMEDA

Walk down the hill along Diego Palacios (Santa Rita) to reach the waterfront and the **Parque Alameda** ❻. This area was given a facelift and completely redesigned in 2015 by

José Martí mausoleum, Cementerio Santa Ifigenia

the Chinese to celebrate the 500th anniversary of the founding of the city. The new *malecón* is a lovely place to stroll or sit overlooking the water. A very popular micro-brewery, **Cervecería Puerto del Rey** (see 4), offers ice cream and food as well as beer in many forms and sizes in a converted warehouse. There is a woman dressed in naval uniform selling tickets here and in the area for boat tours around the harbor, giving you another perspective of the city. Tours leave at 10am, 1pm and 4pm.

CEMENTERIO SANTA IFIGENIA

Some distance northwest (taxi recommended) is the fascinating **Cementerio Santa Ifigenia** 7 (Avenida Crombet, Reparto Juan G Gómez; tel: 22-632 723; 8am–6pm). Once segregated by race and social class, the cemetery has both massive mausoleums and unpretentious graves. Carlos Manuel de Céspedes, Emilio Bacardí, and Compay Segundo (of Buena Vista Social Club fame) are buried here, among other notable figures.

The tombs to receive most visitors, though, are those of Fidel Castro Ruz (1926–2016), whose ashes are interred in a simple boulder with a plaque marked 'Fidel', and of José Martí, whose marble vault has the figures of six women around the outside bearing the symbols of Cuba's provinces at the time. Buried within the

mausoleum is earth from each of the Latin American countries inspired by Martí to assist in the independence struggle. The two are close together and if visiting them, it is worth waiting for the changing of the guard every half hour, accompanied by martial music. The remains of 38 of the Moncada rebels are also buried here, in a special wall just inside the cemetery entrance.

CASTILLO DEL MORRO

To the south of the city, perched above the Bahía de Santiago, is the Spanish fortress: **Castillo de San Pedro de la Roca del Morro** 8, a World Heritage Site housing the **Museo de la Piratería** (tel: 22-691 569; daily 8am–8pm). It is

Guards at the cemetery

The sweeping view from Castillo del Morro

best reached by taxi, unless you have a rental car. The Ruta Turística runs along the shore of the Bahía de Santiago from the city, passing the marina at Punta Gorda and the port of Ciudadmar, close to the fortress, where ferries depart to Cayo Granma and La Socapa in the estuary.

Construction of this stunning fortress began in 1638, to a design by the Italian architect, Juan Bautista Antonelli, son of the man who built El Morro in Havana. It was destroyed in 1662 by the English and rebuilt between 1690 and 1710. It has an elaborate labyrinth of drawbridges, passageways, staircases, and barracks, all executed with precise angles and a geometric beauty. The views across the bay and along the coast are splendid.

Food and Drink

① ISABELICA

Aguilera esq Porfirio Valente, Plaza Dolores; 9am–9pm $

Several flavors of coffee served in this no-frills café. There is food, but the coffee is the star. Rocío del Gallo is the local specialty, a blend of coffee and rum, while Café Isabelica is coffee, rum, and honey. Cubans like to come here for their coffee and a chat, and in the evenings there is Afro-Cuban music.

② CAFÉ CONSTANTIN

Aguilera 2 entre Calvario y Reloj, Plaza Dolores; 9am–9pm; $

Seating in a smart, modern, air-conditioned room if you need to get out of the heat, for coffee, snacks, sweets, and ice cream. For an after-dinner coffee, try Bembito Bomban, which includes cacao liqueur and cinnamon. Víctor Constantin was a French farmer who came from Haiti with his black slave, Isabel María, with whom he was in love, and bought land to grow coffee in the mountains.

③ EL HOLANDÉS

Heredia entre San Félix y el Callejón; tel: 22-624 878; daily noon–11pm; $$

Ideally located only one block from Parque Céspedes and so always full. The restaurant is in a colonial house with the options of sitting in the large dining room, patio with lots of plants, or on the balcony overlooking the Casa de la Trova and listening to their music if you don't mind road noise. The food is acceptable and the service is friendly.

④ CERVECERÍA PUERTO DEL REY

Avenida Jesús Menéndez esq Duvergel; tel: 22-669 304; Mon 4pm–midnight, Tue–Sun noon–midnight; $$

On the Alameda in a converted warehouse among the port buildings. The place to go for a variety of beers brewed using Austrian technology. You can also get ice cream upstairs while downstairs they serve food and there is music until midnight.

Baracoa Bay

BARACOA

Baracoa was the first landing site in Cuba of Christopher Columbus and the first settlement founded by Diego Velázquez, yet for centuries it remained isolated, only accessible by sea until the 1960s. Although there are now roads in and out of the town, it remains a quiet backwater, where visitors come for the slow pace of life.

DISTANCE: 2 miles (3 km) of walking; 24 miles (40 km) of driving
TIME: Two days
START: Parque Independencia
END: Playa La Maguana
POINTS TO NOTE: You need a minimum of two days here if you want to do any hiking or other excursions, with a day for gentle sightseeing and the beach and another day for a trip out of town. Guides are mandatory in the National Park and should be arranged on arrival or sign up with a tour agency. Take plenty of water if venturing on a hike and wear appropriate footwear.

Baracoa's isolation meant that it was a refuge for Amerindians escaping Spanish slavery and they survived here longer than elsewhere. There is archaeological evidence of habitation by the Siboney, Taíno, and Guanahatabey groups and many residents in the area have Amerindian ancestry. There is also a strong French influence in architecture and agriculture, as the colonists fled Haiti after the slave uprising, settling in the eastern coastal regions of Cuba. They introduced new techniques for growing coffee and cacao and Baracoa is known for its chocolate.

The road from Santiago and Guantánamo hugs the coast, turning inland at Cajobabo to Baracoa along the hair-raising but well-maintained road built in 1962 over the mountains. Known as **La Farola** (the Beacon), it twists through some fearsomely acute bends. Despite broken crash barriers and warning notices of accidents, the risk is compensated for by the wonderful scenery: magnificent mountain vistas, wild jungle, coconut groves, and coffee and cocoa plantations. At the stopping places with the best photo opportunities, vendors sell fruit and snacks such as *cuchuruchos*: grated, flavored coconut neatly encased in palm leaves. Avoid anything made of polymita snail shells as they are endangered and protected by international law.

A residential street in Baracoa

BARACOA

The name Baracoa is an Amerindian word meaning 'land of water', a reflection of the many rivers in the area as well as the sea and the plentiful rain. The town nestles beneath El Yunque, a flat, anvil-shaped mountain that was described by Columbus in his log. It was founded in 1512 by Diego Velázquez: the first town and for three years the first capital of Cuba, from where the Spanish started their conquest of the rest of the island.

The streets, picturesque in the late afternoon light, are heaven for photographers, with their neat lines of single-story, pastel-colored houses with red-tiled roofs and lush vegetation. The town has suffered major hurricane damage in recent years, particularly on the seafront Malecón, but always picks itself up. Being so far from Havana, Baracoa is off the main tourist trail, but the town's combination of friendly people, attractive scenery, nearby beaches, and distinctive cuisine make it a great place to spend some time. There are a few small hotels and dozens of *casas particulares*, but no large resorts.

PARQUE INDEPENDENCIA

The **Parque Independencia ❶**, also known as Parque Central, is the center of town and always busy. Calle Antonio Maceo runs along the south side and is pedestrianized for a few blocks, where it is called the Boulevard. On the east side is the **Catedral de Nuestra Señora de la Asunción** (Tue–Sat 8am–noon, 2–4pm, Sat 7–9pm, Sun 8am–noon) which was built in 1805 to replace the original destroyed by pirates in 1652.

Parque Independencia

Inside the church is the **Cruz de la Parra** (Cross of the Vine), which Columbus reputedly brought from Spain and planted here. The historic cross has survived pirates, fires, vandals, and other hazards, although relic-hunters have chipped away at the edges and it is now about half the size it used to be. Standing 3 ft (1 m) tall, it is now kept safe in the cathedral with its edges encased in metal. Controversy over its origins persists, but in 1989 carbon dating confirmed that it was planted in Cuban soil in the late 15th century. However, it is made from the native seagrape tree (Cocoloba diversifolia), which could not have been brought from Spain.

CUEVA DEL PARAÍSO

The **Museo Arqueológico** ❷ (Calle Moncada al final; Mon–Fri 8am–5pm, Sat 8am–noon) is tucked away up a narrow path at the end of Calle Moncada, between people's gardens, in the **Cueva del Paraíso**. It contains objects found in and around Baracoa, including a skeleton of a Taíno chief called Guamá, who fought the Spanish for 10 years. There is also a replica of the Taíno Tobacco Idol, found nearby in 1903 and said to be the most important in the Americas. The original is in Havana's Museo Antropológico Montané. Inside the cave are ladders and a spiral staircase to reach different levels and a glorious view from the Mira-dor at the top. There are lots of caves in the area once used by the Taínos, with stalagmites, stalactites, and petroglyphs and the museum runs archaeological tours of the area.

When leaving the cave, bear left along the hillside and you soon come to the Hotel El Castillo. The building was originally a castle, built in 1770 to keep out the British; it later became a prison and more recently a hotel, enjoying panoramic views of the town and the bay. There is a long flight of steps or a steepish slope back down to the town.

Stop at the **Casa del Chocolate** (see ❶) to sample the local hot chocolate, famously served with salt as well as sugar. Head west along any of the streets running parallel with the sea to reach **Fuerte La Punta** (see ❷), an old fortress with holes for cannon to defend the town against pirates, now converted into a restaurant and a good place for lunch.

Museo Arqueológico skeleton

Baracoa is known for its chocolate

PLAYA MAGUANA

Playa Maguana, about 40 minutes' drive (12 miles/20 km) from Baracoa, is many people's favorite beach and a lovely place to spend the afternoon. There's a small hotel, the Villa Maguana, at one end, and a few rustic places to eat lunch if you haven't eaten in town. Trees come down to the beach and seagrape trees grow further along, so there is shade if you want it. If you haven't got a car, a taxi can be arranged, or the tour agencies arrange transfers.

EXCURSIONS

For the fit there are many rewarding hikes in the mountains, particularly in the **Parque Nacional Alejandro de Humboldt**, the greatest of Cuba's national parks with huge biodiversity and many endemic species. An entry fee is payable and a guide is mandatory, so it is best to arrange a full day trip in advance with one of the state tour agencies or privately through your *casa particular*. The forested mountains of the Cuchillas de Moa and the Cuchillas de Toa in the park are indented by many rivers, tumbling into the sea in picturesque bays.

Hiking up the flat-topped **El Yunque** is a popular activity, although like all walks here, it's hot and sweaty and you will need to carry plenty of water and wear appropriate footwear. The path can get muddy and slippery and it takes at least two hours to get to the top. You start early from the Campismo Popular, about 4 miles (9 km) northwest of Baracoa, to avoid the worst of the heat. Halfway up is a stall selling fruit, which makes a pleasant break. From the top you can see all along the coast. There are endemic plants up here which grow nowhere else. On your descent you have the option to bathe in waterfalls or swim in the Río Duaba.

Food and Drink

① CASA DEL CHOCOLATE
Maceo esq Maraví; $
Baracoa is the center of cacao growing in Cuba and all the best chocolate comes from this region. Although your *casa particular* will offer hot chocolate for breakfast, come here for the more savory version, made with cocoa, water, sugar, and salt. There is also chocolate ice cream, snacks, cakes and sweets, all charged in Cuban pesos and cheap.

② FUERTE LA PUNTA
Avenida de los Mártires; tel: 21-641 480; daily 10am–10pm; $$
The fort at La Punta at the west end of town is a great location for lunch, looking out over the bay. The restaurant here is open air and reasonably priced, offering anything from sandwiches to pasta, chicken, or fish in coconut milk.

DIRECTORY

Hand-picked hotels and restaurants to suit all budgets and tastes, organised by area, plus select nightlife listings, an alphabetical listing of practical information, a language guide, and an overview of the best books and films to give you a flavor of the island.

Rooftop pool at the Gran Hotel Manzana Kempinski La Habana

ACCOMMODATIONS

Hotels are run by state enterprises, and you can ascertain the standard of the hotel from the name of the enterprise. Hotels run by Islazul tend to be two-star or three-star, while those run by Gran Caribe or Cubanacán are often four-star, although the star rating does not equate with what you'd expect in a hotel abroad.

In Old Havana there are delightful boutique hotels in renovated mansions. They come in a variety of sizes, ages, and prices, but all can be booked online at www.gaviotahotels.com. In other towns, look for the Hoteles E chain of boutique hotels in converted colonial mansions. In the resorts and in Havana, there are joint-venture hotels run by foreign companies.

Staying in a private house (*casa particular*) can be the most rewarding way of experiencing Cuba. Not only do you get to know the owners, but there is usually a better standard of service, cleanliness, and comfort than in the equivalent or higher value of hotel room. The food served is fresher and often cooked better, while special diets can be accommodated on request. Personal safety is excellent and theft is rare. *Casas particulares* must be registered with the authorities and should display a blue, anchor-shaped sign on or above the front door. Cuban hosts must fill out a form with visitors' details, and present it to the police.

In high season it is best to reserve rooms in advance and always reconfirm your booking the day before you get there.

Old Havana

Conde de Ricla Hostal

San Ignacio 402 e/. Sol y Muralla; tel: 7-862 7461; www.condedericlahostal.com; $$

This conversion of an old building just off Plaza Vieja offers four rooms and one suite ($$$), all to a high modern standard. Privately-run, the service is friendly and efficient. A complimentary breakfast is served in an independent restaurant downstairs, while the rooftop terrace is perfect for chilling out in the evening.

El Balcón Colonial de Yamelis

Cuba 518 e/. Muralla y Teniente Rey; tel: 5331 9498; fllanes@gmail.com; $

A block from Plaza Vieja, Yamelis offers two rooms in an apartment with high ceilings and huge windows and balcony overlooking the street. Each has a private bathroom, air conditioning, fan, safe box, and fridge. A good breakfast is provided on request.

Price for a standard double room for one night without breakfast in high season:
$ = below $40
$$ = $40–100
$$$ = $100–200
$$$$ = above $200

Hotel Nacional

Gran Hotel Manzana Kempinski La Habana

San Rafael e/. Monserrate y Zulueta; tel: 7-869 9100; www.kempinski.com; $$$$
Luxury hotel on the Parque Central. Get a park-facing room for best views; others overlook shops. Service is spotty but the location and facilities can't be beaten. Glorious rooftop bar, pool, and spa.

Vista al Prado

Cárcel 156 Apto 3 e/. San Lázaro y Prado; tel: 7-861 7817; www.vistalpradohavana.com; $
Good sized rooms with tiled floors and air conditioning, Wi-Fi, wall safe, plenty of hot water and helpful, English-speaking hosts who offer a good, filling breakfast. The apartment is up 64 stairs, but in a great location round the corner from the Prado and the Malecón.

Vedado

Casa Betty y Armando Gutiérrez

Calle 21 62 Apto 7 e/. M y N; tel: 7-832 1876; arbehabana@gmail.com; $
Lovely apartment in the 4th-floor penthouse with direct elevator access, close to restaurants and nightlife. Armando and Betty are very knowledgeable on history and culture, speak English and have been renting two rooms for over 20 years.

Casa Jorge Coalla Potts

Ave I 456 Apto 11 e/. 21 y 23; tel: 7-832 9032; www.havanaroomsrental.com; $
Jorge and Marisel are among the most experienced hosts in all Cuba. Rooms are clean and beds are comfortable; there is plenty of hot water and a fridge for your drinks. The location is quiet yet only a short walk from most sights in Vedado.

Hotel Nacional de Cuba

Calle 21 y O; tel: 7-836 3564; www.hotelnacionaldecuba.com; $$$$
Most people who stay at this iconic, waterfront hotel are on packages and rarely pay the advertised rate. Dating from 1930, the architecture is superb, but there is an air of faded grandeur and some rooms need renovating. Perched on the clifftop in gardens, it is a great place to sit and take in the view.

Meliá Cohiba

Paseo entre 1 y 3; tel: 7-833 3636; www.meliacuba.com; $$$$
A high rise on the seafront of an international standard with good service and most of its 460 rooms have sea views. Filled to bursting with restaurants, cafés, bars, nightclubs, and shops, as well as a gym and a swimming pool.

Sierra del Rosario (Las Terrazas, Soroa)

Casa Hospedaje Villa Duque

Finca San Andrés, road to Cayajabos, 1 mile/ 2km from Las Terrazas; tel: 5322 1431; $
Delightful rural location on the family farm and almost all the food is home grown. English is spoken by family members, who are helpful and informative. They have a 1955 Chevy for transportation and local excursions.

Room at the Meliá Cohiba

Casa Los Sauces

Carretera a Soroa Km 3; tel: 5228 9372;
lossauces@nauta.cu; $
On the road up to the Orchidarium in a
peaceful, rural position. Ana Lidia works
in the Orchidarium and has created her
own beautiful garden, which is managed
by husband Jorge and English-speaking
son, Tito, who also offers transportation.

Hotel Moka

Las Terrazas; tel: 48-578 600;
www.hotelmoka-lasterrazas.com; $$
Built in and around trees with lovely views,
a peaceful atmosphere and a swimming
pool, this small eco-hotel is used mostly
by groups and packages are available.
Staff are very knowledgeable and can
arrange guided walks and birdwatching.

Viñales

Casa Deborah Susana

Calle C Final 1, tel: 48-796 207;
deborahsusana7@nauta.cu; $
Central but tucked away and very quiet.
The helpful hosts can arrange excursions
and provide tasty meals and cocktails.
Independent access for guests and a
leafy patio with a hammock. Parking.

Casa El Cafetal

Calle Adela Azcuy Norte Final; tel: 5331
1752; see Facebook; $
The last house on the road as you head
out of town, peaceful, rural and with
lovely views. The family can arrange
horse riding or mountain climbing and
will look after you well, with great food.

Horizontes Los Jazmines

Carretera a Viñales Km 23; tel: 48-796 205;
www.cubanacan.cu; $$$
Outside town on a hillside with a glori-
ous view over the valley. Rooms are OK
but food is better at local *paladares* down
the road. Similarly, walk 400 yds/m to the
information center to book tours cheaper
than at the hotel. Nice pool with a view.

Zapata Peninsula

Hostal Luís

Carretera a Cienfuegos esq Carretera a
Playa Larga, Playa Girón; tel: 5238 1264;
hostalluis@yahoo.es; $
Seven rooms and suites in the main house
or adjacent building, all with independent
access and well maintained. The restaurant serves superb seafood. Dinner, bed
and breakfast packages available. Excursions and diving can be arranged. Parking.

Kiki Hostal

Barrio Caletón, Playa Larga; tel: 45-987
404; www.hostalkiki.com; $
Right on the beach and one of the more
expensive *casas* in Cuba, but worth it.
The upstairs room is the larger, with
a sea view, but costs more and is a bit
tricky to get up to with luggage. Kiki is
helpful and can arrange tours.

Cienfuegos

Bella Perla Marina

Calle 39 5818 esq 60; tel: 43-518 991;
wrodriguezdelrey@yahoo.es; $
There are two internal rooms that are nice
enough, but the star is the suite upstairs

Pool at the Meliá Cohiba

($$; sleeps six): light and bright with one huge bed and two others in a loft, with a great bathroom and Jacuzzi. Food is served upstairs on a lovely terrace, huge breakfasts, and delicious dinners. Waldo and Amileidis are attentive hosts.

Palacio Azul
Calle 37 1202 e/. 12 y 14, Punta Gorda; tel: 43-555 828; www.gran-caribe.com; $$$
This charming powder-blue boutique hotel has only seven rooms but stands out for its service and architecture. It's a long walk into town, but closer to the tip of the peninsula and the Yacht Club. Breakfast only although there's a bar for drinks and snacks. Roof terrace overlooking the sea.

Casa Muñoz
José Martí 401 e/. Fidel Claro y Santiago Escobar; tel: 41-993 673; www.casa. trinidadphoto.com; $$
An historic house, built in 1800 with high ceilings and tiled floors, sensitively renovated into two standard rooms or one suite on two levels for family groups. English speaking, Julio Muñoz is a knowledgeable host who runs photography workshops. The family has dogs and horse riding can be arranged. Parking.

Casa Rogelio Inchauspi Bastida
Simón Bolívar 312 e/. José Martí y Antonio Maceo; tel: 41-994 107; $$
Formerly the Spanish Consulate, this grand old colonial house is full of antiques and period details. The rooms are cool and spacious with high ceilings but air conditioning is available. There is a lovely roof terrace with gorgeous views. Rogelio and Barbara are charming hosts.

Iberostar Grand Hotel Trinidad
José Martí y Lino Pérez; tel: 41-996 070; www.iberostar.com; $$$
Splendid renovated colonial building with a green and white façade overlooking Parque Céspedes. The rooms and suites are comfortable, but there's no pool or external patio. No children under 15.

Casa Mercy
San Cristóbal (E Machado) 4 e/. Cuba y Colón; tel: 42-216 941; casamercy@gmail.com; $
Omelio and Mercedes Moreno run this excellent, modernized *casa*. Guest rooms are separate from the family quarters, upstairs with access to a roof terrace. Good food, any diet catered for, good cocktails and rum tasting too. The family also runs Casa Mercy 1938, at Independencia (Bulevar) 253 e/. Unión y San Isidro, with a central courtyard and two bright rooms.

Hostal Florida Terrace
Candelaria (Maestra Nicolasa) 59 e/. Colón y Maceo; tel: 42-221 580; florida.terrace@yahoo.com; $
Modern *hostal* furnished in Art Deco style, with six light and airy rooms, each with two beds, air conditioning and hot showers. There is a great terrace with a bar and sunbathing area. Owner Angel Martínez Rodríguez also runs Hostal Florida Center

The superb valley views from Horizontes Los Jazmines, Viñales

across the road (Candelaria 56), a colonial house with rooms full of antiques and a fabulous restaurant (see page 109).

Remedios and Cays

Hostal Buen Viaje
Andrés del Río 20 e/. Enrique Malaret y Máximo Gómez, Remedios; tel: 42-396 560; hostal.buenviaje@gmail.com; $
A colonial house with a pretty patio garden and fountain. The rooms have high ceilings and air conditioning. Owners Lester and Naty are friendly, helpful, and offer great food. Parking. A second, colonial house with five bedrooms is due to open in 2018.

Hotel E Camino del Príncipe
Camilo Cienfuegos 9 e/. Montalván y Alejandro del Río; tel: 42-395 144; www.cubanacan.cu; $$$
A charming old mansion on two floors overlooking the square. 26 rooms with air conditioning and good facilities including nice showers. Try and get an outside room with a window as the interior rooms can be stuffy.

Villa Las Brujas
Cayo Las Brujas; tel: 42-350 199; www.gaviota-grupo.com; $$$
A small hotel perched up above the beach and the only one on the cays that isn't all-inclusive. 24 wooden *cabañas* with verandas and balconies are connected by a boardwalk; get one with a sea view as they are better. Don't expect luxury and not everything works, but it is a wonderful location by a superb beach with the marina in walking distance for water activities.

Camagüey

Casa Miriam
Joaquín de Agüero 525 e/. 25 de Julio y Perucho Figueredo, Reparto La Vigía; tel: 32-282 120; miriamhous29@yahoo.com; $
In a quiet area, this modern house offers two spacious, airy rooms. Large, leafy roof terrace. Miriam speaks English and is a helpful, knowledgeable host. Parking.

Hospedaje Colonial Los Vitrales
Avellaneda 3 e/. Gen Gómez y Martí; tel: 32-295 866; requejobarreto@gmail.com; $
Rafael Requejo and his family run this colonial house with three rooms overlooking a patio. His sister has a suite to rent through the garage and his son has a modern *hostal* across the road. Central, with experienced hosts.

Hotel E El Marqués
Cisneros 222 e/. Hermanos Agüero y Martí; tel: 32-244 937; www.cubanacan.cu; $$$
A stylish six-room boutique hotel in a beautiful old building with a central patio. There is a bar but no restaurant (lots of *paladares* nearby). The staff are welcoming and the rooms are well-equipped.

Parque Nacional Sierra Maestra (Bayamo & Santo Domingo)

Casa Arturo y Esmeralda
Zenea 56 entre William Soler y Capote, Bayamo; tel: 23-424 051; casabayamo@nauta.cu; $
Accommodates 16 guests and is known for its helpful hosts: Arturo going the extra

mile to arrange trips or transportation, and Esmeralda cooks up a feast at any hour.

Mirador de Arcadia
Santo Domingo; tel: 5858 0202; $
On a hillside with a wonderful view over the forest. There are three rooms, each with two or three beds and private bathroom. Good home cooking – welcome if you are hiking in the mountains. Arcadia can arrange hikes to Pico Turquino (with notice) and Comandancia de la Plata.

Santiago de Cuba
Casa Dulce
Bartolomé Masó (San Basilio) 552 Altos esq Clarín; tel: 22-625 479; gdcastillo20@yahoo.es; $
A corner apartment with one large, comfortable bedroom. The living room has huge windows and the lovely roof terrace has great views. Charming host Gladys Domenech speaks some English.

Casa Granda
Heredia 201 e/. San Pedro y San Félix, Parque Céspedes; tel: 22-653 021; www.cubanacan.cu; $$$
A hotel since 1914, and a celebrity haunt ever since, it now exudes an air of faded grandeur. Some of the rooms are in need of a facelift, others suffer from music going on late into the night. Great rooftop bar, terrace bar and café, and a disco.

Casa Mayita
San Basilio 472 Altos esq Reloj; tel: 22-658 973; kath_bateman@hotmail.com; $
A first-floor apartment with balcony. Huge windows and doors make it light and airy. Roof terrace with views of the bay and mountains. Two rooms, each with two beds. Meals are available, although there are lots of *paladares* nearby.

Baracoa
Casa Andrés Cruzata Rigores
Wilder Galano Reyes 23 Altos e/. Abel Díaz Delgado y Ramón López Peña; tel: 21-642 697; cruzata.bacoa2012@yahoo.es; $
The family lives downstairs while the two guest rooms and sitting room are upstairs, each with a fully stocked fridge and air conditioning. Roof terrace. The helpful owners can arrange tours and their daughter speaks several languages.

Hostal La Habanera
Maceo esq Frank País; tel: 21-645 273; www.gaviota-grupo.com; $$
Ten rooms in this central boutique hotel close to all the nightlife. There is a bar and restaurant and lots of *paladares* close by too. Rooms are air-conditioned, staff are helpful, tours can be booked. Wi-Fi.

Hotel Villa Maguana
Carretera a Moa Km 20; tel: 21-641 204; www.gaviota-grupo.com; $$$
12 miles (19 km) from Baracoa, this is one of the few beach hotels not all-inclusive and the only place to stay on a beach in this area. There are 16 rooms, a poor restaurant, beach bar, and little else. Private beach. Walk to the public beach to find *paladares* for better food.

The famous La Guarida

RESTAURANTS

Nobody goes to Cuba for the food and it has the reputation of being bland and stodgy. Nevertheless, the standard Cuban meal will usually consist of pork or chicken accompanied by rice, beans, another starchy vegetable such as yucca or plantain, and a salad of shredded cabbage, sliced tomato, cucumber, and other vegetables such as green beans.

Restaurants in Havana are more varied than elsewhere. There are Spanish restaurants offering *garbanzos* (chickpeas) and *paella*, Italian restaurants offering pizza and pasta or Chinese restaurants in Chinatown cooking a rather sweet version of Oriental cuisine. *Paladares* in Havana are often more innovative. The best require reservations as they are so popular.

Old Havana

Café del Oriente
Oficios 112 esq Amargura, Plaza de San Francisco; tel: 7-860 6686; daily noon–midnight; $$$
Very elegant white-tablecloth establishment – the most upmarket in Old Havana.

> Prices are for a two-course meal, not including drinks.
> $ = less than $10
> $$ = $10–20
> $$$ = $20–40
> $$$$ = $40 and up

Here you can get chateaubriand and other cuts of beef which are tender and tasty, but there are also Cuban specialties, all at very reasonable prices considering the smart location. Tables outside are nice for lunch or drinks before dinner, when you move inside, upstairs or downstairs, to be serenaded by musicians.

Los Nardos (Sociedad Juventud Asturiana)
Paseo de Martí (Prado) 563 e/. Dragones y Teniente Rey; tel: 7-863 2985; $$
This quirky, popular place has a busy, buzzing atmosphere. No reservations taken, so you have to wait in a well-regulated line outside. Good wine list. Huge portions, of pork, lamb, Uruguayan beef, chicken, fish, shrimp, and lobster with all the trimmings. The service is efficient and friendly. You don't have to queue if you go to the restaurants upstairs: El Trofeo, which serves Cuban and international food, or El Asturianito, serving Cuban and Italian food, with good pizzas.

Hanoi
Teniente Rey 507 y Bernaza; tel: 7-867 1029; $
Despite the name, the food is *criolla*. Lots of pork, chicken, shrimp, cheap and cheerful, although you can get lobster for CUC$15, three times the price of most dishes. Cheap cocktails, live music, and a relaxed atmosphere.

Friendly waiter at Café del Oriente

La Guarida

Concordia 418 e/. Gervasio y Escobar, Centro; tel: 7-866 9047; www.laguarida.com; $$$

You must book well in advance, as this *paladar* featured in the famous Cuban film *Fresa y Chocolate* – or, rather, the film featured the crumbling tenement building, and the *paladar* followed two years later. It is always full with tourists and if a tour party is in service suffers. The décor is kitsch and eclectic, the food is varied and excellent, and portions are "nouveau" without being small. The prices are high, as the restaurant trades on its movie connections, but it is worth a visit.

San Cristóbal

San Rafael 469 e/. Lealtad y Campanario, Centro; tel: 7-860 1705; $$$

Famous for having hosted the Obama family when they visited Cuba in 2016. They ate here for good reason, the food is good, well presented, and the multilingual service is excellent. A lovely old building and beautiful restaurant, the walls filled with paintings, clocks, and memorabilia. Reservations are essential. The platter of starters is magnificent. Rum and cigars follow an excellent meal.

Vedado

La Torre

17 55 e/. My N, Edificio Focsa; tel: 7-838 3089; $$$

Up on the 33rd floor with a glorious view over Havana. The bar faces west for sunset cocktails, which are excellent, the dining room faces the Hotel Nacional and Old Havana for a romantic view at night. Open from noon until midnight, it is worth coming any time of day for a drink, snack, or meal. Good food, friendly service.

Café Laurent

M 257 e/. 19 y 21; tel: 7-831 2090; on Facebook; $$$

A very upmarket *paladar*, modern and elegant, with efficient service and a high standard of fusion cuisine, the closest you'll come to fine dining. Located in the penthouse, you come out of the elevator into the dining room which has wonderful views over Havana from the huge windows and the terrace.

Le Chansonnier

J 257 e/. 15 y Línea; tel: 7-832 1576; www.lechansonnierhabana.com; $$$

A very elegant restaurant in a handsome Vedado mansion, with tall windows and doors and high ceilings hung with chandeliers. The food and multilingual service are among the best in Havana.

Starbien

29 205 e/. B y C; tel: 7-830 0711; $$

One of the best restaurants in Cuba, serving innovative fusion food at reasonable prices. A five-course lunch special is only CUC$12, while most mains are around CUC$8–14. You can pay more for a steak, but there are more interesting choices, such as octopus carpaccio or sesame marlin with teriyaki sauce. Excellent service, eat in the air-conditioned dining room or in the garden; reservations advised.

Al fresco drinks

La Cocina de Lilliam

48 1311 e/. 13 y 15, Miramar; tel: 7-209 6514; $$$

Lovely setting in a pretty garden. Very good and tasty Cuban and Spanish-influenced dishes, which are popular so reservations are recommended. Home-made bread and ice cream with unusual flavors.

Sierra del Rosario (Las Terrazas, Soroa)

La Fonda de Mercedes, Edificio 9, Apto 2, Las Terrazas; tel: 48-578647; $$

A good place to come for typical Cuban food. The *ropa vieja* is tasty and tender and comes with the usual accompaniments of yuca, rice and beans, and vegetables. As with the other places in Las Terrazas, tour parties can descend and take up the limited space, so it is often best to eat early or late. Open 9am–9pm.

Viñales

3 J Bar de Tapas (Tres Jotas)

Salvador Cisneros 45; tel: 48-793 334; $$

A modern tapas bar in a renovated old house where you can sit indoors or on the veranda. The staff are very friendly and will customize your rum cocktail on request. Most tapas are priced CUC$3–8 and portions are good.

Buena Vista

Carretera a Hotel Los Jazmines; tel: 5223 8616; $$

A very pleasant setting with a glorious view over the Viñales valley. The food is good and the portions plentiful – even

the lobster is good. Sit on the veranda for the best views.

El Olivo

Salvador Cisneros 89; tel: 48-696 654; $$

This Mediterranean *paladar* is a welcome change from rice and beans. Good fish, pasta, paella, and even cheese. The service is slow but the food is tasty. Queues outside are testament to its popularity.

Zapata Peninsula

Chuchi El Pescador

Playa Larga, a short walk from where the buses stop. $$

Very fresh fish, with some interesting varieties, depending on the catch. Also lobster, crab, shrimp, and a mixed seafood platter if you can't make up your mind. Main dishes come with all the usual trimmings: rice, plantain, salads. Nothing out of the ordinary, but well presented.

La Terraza de Mily

Opposite Hotel Playa Larga; tel: 45-987 375; $

Mily and Alain provide good home cooking, nothing fancy but fresher and tastier than anything served at the hotel opposite, so guests migrate here for a decent meal and a warm welcome.

Cienfuegos

Aché

Avenida 38 4106 e/. 41 y 43; tel: 43-526 173; $$

A long-established, professional *paladar* serving generous cocktails and Spanish

A typical pork dish

and Chilean wine. The specialty is shrimp, but it is all good, with friendly service.

Casa Prado
Calle 37 4626 e/. 46 y 48; tel: 5262 3858; $$
Good food and large portions, including lovely fresh fish and seafood. Attentive service. Reservations needed for groups as there are often queues outside.

Te Quedarás
Ave 54 (Bulevar) 3509 e/. 35 y 37; tel: 5826 1283; $$
The elegant dining room and bar is upstairs in a grand colonial house with a lovely balcony where you can sit and watch the world go by. The menu is varied and there are pasta and vegetarian options to make a change from *comida criolla*.

Trinidad

Estela
Simón Bolívar 557; tel: 41-994 329; $$
A family-run *paladar* and one of the most popular places to eat in town, so get there early. Tables in the walled garden. Food is fresh and tasty with lots of choice and plentiful portions, including heaps of avocado from the tree in the garden in season. Lamb is the house specialty. Friendly hosts, good service. Open Mon–Fri 6.30–9.30pm only.

Guitarra Mía
Jesús Menéndez 19 e/. Lino Pérez y Camilo Cienfuegos; $$
Hand-decorated guitars adorn the walls and the music theme is carried through to the food presentation, with guitar-shaped vegetables and musical symbols drawn on the plates. A cosy, intimate *paladar*, serving good food with pleasant service and, of course, live music.

La Ceiba
Pablo Pich Girón 263 e/. Lino Pérez y Independencia; tel: 41-992 408; $$
The ceiba is the huge old tree in the courtyard, around which tables are placed and the setting is lovely, particularly at night. The food is good, a mixture of Cuban food with more international dishes, depending on the availability of ingredients.

La Redacción
Maceo 463 e/. Simón Bolívar y Francisco J Zerquera; tel: 994 593; www.laredaccion cuba.com; $$
The house was formerly the office of a newspaper, hence the décor. The food is mostly Cuban with vegetarian options such as crêpes and veggie burgers.

San José
Maceo 382 entre Colón y Smith; tel: 41-994 702; www.sanjosetaste.com; $$
Very good bar and restaurant in colonial style with lovely old tiled floor. The menu features Cuban dishes as well as pizza, pasta, sandwiches, and ice cream; something for all the family.

Santa Clara

Florida Center
Maestra Nicolasa (Candelaria) 56 e/. Colón y Maceo; tel: 42-208 161; $$

Tamale, Cuban-style

Reservations are advised for this lovely restaurant in the courtyard of a colonial house where you are surrounded by lush foliage and orchids in a very romantic setting, accompanied by live music. The food is very good and tasty, whether it is *ropa vieja* or lobster and there are lots of options such as smoked pork and delicious sauces to make a change from the usual *comida criolla*.

La Casona Guevara

J B Zayas 160 e/. E Machado (San Cristóbal) y Candelaria; tel: 42-224 279; $$
Another colonial house with a patio and live music. Huge plates of colorful food with a wide range of vegetables are attractively presented and there are options for vegetarians.

La Aldaba

Luís Estévez 61 e/. Independencia (Bulevar) y Martí; tel: 42-208 686; $$
A restaurant and bar on the roof terrace above a *casa particular*, La Auténtica Pérgola, you can come here for breakfast, lunch, dinner, or just drinks, although reservations are advised for food. It is romantic at night when there is live music.

Remedios

Taberna los Siete Juanes

Máximo Gómez esq Parque Central; $$
A very attractive wine and tapas bar on the corner of the main square with tables outside or inside. A lovely place to relax with a drink and some tasty food, watching the world go by.

Driver's Bar

Camilo Cienfuegos esq José Antonio Peña; $
This bar is the focal point for a club of vintage car owners and has been popular for the people-to-people experiences when drivers assemble with their cars and motorbikes and visitors get a ride.

Camagüey

Casa Austria

Lugareño e/. San Rafael y San Clemente; tel: 5328 5580; $$
Chef Josef runs this rare Austrian restaurant in the patio of a colonial house and he is known for his pastries and sweets, worth buying even if you don't eat here. The food is as authentic as he can manage given the difficulties in finding the right ingredients and is a welcome change.

Casa Italia

San Ramón 11 e/. Gen Gómez y Astilleros; tel: 32-257 614; $$
A good place to come for pizza baked in a wood-fired oven and eaten in a courtyard garden. The other menu items are fairly standard and not particularly Italian.

Parador de los Tres Reyes

Plaza San Juan de Dios; tel: 32-286 812; $$
This is the cheaper of the two Spanish restaurants on the Plaza San Juan de Dios. Often busy with tour parties at lunchtime, it is nevertheless an attractive place to come for dinner.

Campana de Toledo

Plaza San Juan de Dios; tel: 32-286 812; $$$

Courtyard dining in Santiago

A Spanish restaurant with tables overlooking the Plaza San Juan de Dios or in the courtyard. Like its neighbor, it is busy at lunchtime with day-trippers, so best to come at night.

Bayamo

San Salvador
Maceo 107 e/. Donato Mármol y Martí; tel: 23-426 942; $$
In a large, colonial house with high ceilings and tall doorways. A wide choice of local, well-prepared dishes.

Restauran Vegetariano
Gen García esq Bartolomé Masó; $
Open daily from noon until midnight, this is a good, cheap place to come for vegetarian food, with a wide choice of dishes.

Santiago de Cuba

El Palenquito
Avenida del Río 28 e/. Calle 6 y Carretera del Caney, Reparto Pastorita; tel: 22-645 220; on Facebook; $$
A cab ride east of the center, this is a lovely open-air restaurant under a thatched roof in a garden. Much of the meat or seafood is cooked to order on the grill, but there are plenty of other dishes. Service is good and so are the drinks, including the coffee.

La Bendita Farándula
Barnada 513 e/. Aguilera y Heredia; tel: 22-653 739; $$
At the entrance, bear left for this small *paladar* specializing in surf and turf, *mar y tierra*. Lots of seafood on offer as well as

the regular chicken and pork, nicely presented but with mixed levels of service.

St Pauli
Enramada 605 e/. Barnada y Plácido; tel: 22-652 292; $$
The food is good and the menu extensive. After midnight, and after they stop serving food, it converts to a lounge bar.

Setos Cuba
Av Manduley 154 e/. 9 y 11, Reparto Vista Alegre; tel: 5355 2204; $$$
Away from the center, the restaurant is in an elegant suburban mansion and generally considered to be among the best in Santiago. Owned by a Spaniard married to a Cuban, you can expect authentic Spanish dishes using Spanish olive oil and accompanied by Spanish wines, although there is Cuban food as well.

Baracoa

Al's
Calixto García 158A e/. Céspedes y Galano; tel: 21-642 658; $$
Lovely location perched up on the hillside on an upstairs terrace with views over the town and bay. Much of the food is cooked on the barbeque, particularly good if you like lobster and shrimp.

La Cacha Pizzería
Martí 176 Altos e/. Céspedes y Ciro Frías; tel: 5339 5900; $$
Come here for pizza baked in a wood-fired oven or pasta. You can eat inside or outdoors with the added advantage of Wi-Fi.

Cabaret Parisien in Havana

NIGHTLIFE

While Havana has the most varied and plentiful nightlife, with bars, clubs, dance venues, theaters, concert halls and cinemas offering a huge range of music and cultural activities, every town in Cuba is well provided with the arts. You will find a Casa de la Música and/or a Casa de la Trova, for traditional music, in every town. Cultural events and concerts take place in a Casa de la Cultura and there is usually a Patio de Artex, a bar/café with an open-air space where you can hear contemporary music and comedy.

Havana's nightlife scene is constantly changing but your hotel or *casa particular* will be able to advise you on venues. www.lahabana.com is a monthly online guide to what's on in the capital, occasionally covering festivals and events in other cities as well. EGREM publishes a *cartelera* of what's on at Casas de la Música and other state cultural venues, http://promociones.egrem.co.cu.

Cabaret

Havana

Parisien

Hotel Nacional, O esq 21, Vedado; tel: 7-873 3564.

Cheaper than the Tropicana, this show in the Nacional lasts longer and is equally good. Open 9pm–2.30am; show starts at 10pm; reservations required.

Tropicana

Calle 72 4504 e/. 43 y 45, Marianao; tel: 70267 1717.

This is the most elaborate and impressive of Cuba's cabarets. Any hotel tourism bureau will book seats for you, but the show is expensive; tickets CUC$75–95 depending on your seat; a tour will include transport, which can be CUC$12 by cab. Open air – it is canceled if it rains. Open until 2am.

Turquino

Hotel Habana Libre, 23 esq L, Vedado; tel: 7-834 6100.

Disco on the 25th floor, with occasional live salsa from top groups. The roof opens and you can dance under the stars. Open daily 10.30pm–3am, cabaret 11pm and 1am.

Santiago de Cuba

Club Tropicana Santiago

Autopista Nacional Km 1.5; tel: 22-642 579. Santiago puts its stamp on this glitzy show, with local touches to distinguish it from its Havana namesake. Open 8pm–3am with disco after the show; tickets cost around CUC$30, but packages are available that include transportation and drinks.

Santiago Café

Hotel Meliá Santiago de Cuba, Avenida las Américas.

The Gran Teatro de La Habana Alicia Alonso

This is a smart nightclub with cabaret, live music and disco, very popular so get there early if you don't want to queue. Open 9pm–3am.

Classical and modern dance

Havana

Gran Teatro de la Habana Alicia Alonso

Paseo de Martí (Prado) 458 esq San Rafael, Parque Central; tel: 7-861 3077.

Directed since its creation in 1961 by Alicia Alonso (1920-), the National Ballet of Cuba (Ballet Nacional de Cuba) is world famous for its fluid grace and technique. The company is often on tour, but when at home it performs here or at the Teatro Nacional de Cuba. You can also see here performances by Acosta Danza, the contemporary dance company, incorporating influences of folklore and urban dance, set up by Carlos Acosta in 2016 on his return to Cuba from dancing with the Royal Ballet Company in the UK. When not touring abroad, his company, based at Línea 857 e/. 4 y 6, Vedado; tel: 7-833 5699; www.acostadanza.com, can be seen rehearsing through the large windows of the studio.

Teatro Nacional de Cuba

Paseo y 39, Plaza de la Revolución; tel: 7-879 3558.

Cuba's impressive Contemporary Dance Company (Danza Contemporánea de Cuba) performs avant-garde and other forms of modern dance. Its base is here but performances can also be seen as the Sala Hubert de Blanck.

Sala Hubert de Blanck

Calzada 654 e/. A y B, Vedado; tel: 7-830 1011.

Contemporary dance companies perform here but it is principally a venue for classical and contemporary music concerts, while it has also staged major works of drama.

Camagüey

Teatro Principal

Padre Valencia 64; tel: 32-293 048.

The city has its own highly-rated ballet company, the Ballet de Camagüey, which can be seen performing here.

Jazz clubs

Havana

Jazz Café

Galerías de Paseo, Paseo esq Ave Primera, Vedado; tel: 7-838 2696.

A famous jazz club, frequented by Chucho Valdés, with live music (two sets, 9.30pm and 11pm). New groups and lots of improvisation greeted enthusiastically by a knowledgeable audience.

La Zorra y El Cuervo

Calle 23 e/. N y O, Vedado; tel: 7-833 2402.

Famous jazz club on La Rampa in a basement (look for UK-style red phone box at entrance). Live music from 11pm. Open daily 10pm–2am. Entrance of

On stage at La Zorra y El Cuervo jazz club

CUC$10 includes two drinks. Get there early if you want a table as it is small and cosy.

Santiago de Cuba

Iris Jazz Club
Paraíso y Aguilera, Plaza Marte.
Local and national jazz players perform here and it is a great place to hear jazz.

Music and Dance

Havana

1830
Malecón y 20, Vedado, on the waterfront by the Miramar tunnel; tel: 7-838 3090.
Right on the waterfront at the mouth of the Río Almendares, this is a restaurant and bar with cabaret shows Mon–Sat 10pm–3am, Sun 6pm–midnight, live music, and dancing outdoors in a lovely location.

Café Cantante Mi Habana
Basement, Teatro Nacional, Paseo y 39, Plaza de la Revolución; tel: 7-878 4275.
The program varies; sometimes disco, live music of all kinds (usually on weekends), or stand-up (in rapid Spanish). It's a small, lively basement venue and quickly fills up. Open daily 5pm–3am; afternoon and evening performances. Saturday is popular with the LGBT crowd.

Café Teatro Bertolt Brecht
13 e/. I y J, Vedado; tel: 830 1354.
This large basement bar is open nightly but on Tue, Thu and Fri nights there is live music by contemporary, up and coming bands, an event known as No se lo digas a nadie (Don't tell anybody).

El Submarino Amarillo
17 esq 6, Parque John Lennon, Vedado.
A homage to the Beatles, with tribute bands playing golden oldies, not only by the Beatles but also bands like Queen or Led Zeppelin. Heavy metal and rock are very popular. Open Mon 9pm–2am, Tue–Sat 2–7.30pm, 9pm–2am, Sun 2–10pm.

Casa de la Música EGREM, Sala Te Quedarás
20 3308 esq 35, Miramar; tel: 7-204 0447.
Open every day for music and dancing with an early session for youngsters at 5–9pm and a later session from 11pm,

The red phone box outside La Zorra y El Cuervo

Live band entertaining the crowds at a market in Trinidad

while the music shop is open 11am–11pm. All sorts of Havana bands play here and the program changes frequently. Upstairs night owls can hear both traditional and alternative music played in intimate surroundings in Diablo Tun Tun, 11pm–6am.

Don Cangrejo
Av Primera e/. 16 y 18, Miramar; tel: 7-504 5002.
Although this is open daily, it is busiest Fri night when the latest hot bands are playing. It is an open air venue on the waterfront, open 11pm–3am, and the cover charge varies depending on who is playing, about CUC$5–20.

Fábrica de Arte Cubano
Calle 26 esq 11, Vedado; www.fac.cu; Thu–Sun 8pm–3am
This new and innovative cultural center has taken Havana by storm. In a converted cooking oil factory, it is a combination of modern art and design gallery, theatre, live music venue, video, dance floor, bars, and a restaurant, El Cocinero. You can hear all forms of popular music here and it's a must. Come early as queues build up around the block by 9pm and it's packed by 11pm. Entrance CUC$2 and you get a card which is stamped when you buy drinks for payment on leaving.

Humboldt 52
Humboldt 52 e/. Infanta y Hospital; tel: 5295-4893; on Facebook.

Havana's first gay bar also welcomes all orientations and is great fun. There is a dance floor where you can see some hot salsa moves, large screens for music videos, karaoke, drag performances, and sometimes singers.

Salón Rosado Benny Moré, La Tropical
Avenidas 41 y 46, Miramar; tel: 7-206 1282.
The best live salsa venue in Cuba. A big, no-frills outdoor arena. Closed Mon–Thu, then electronic music Fri, 7pm–4am. Sat live bands 8.30pm–3am, cover charge depends on who is playing, Sun 5–11pm.

Viñales

Bar Polo Montañez
Next to the Casa de la Cultura on the plaza.
Live music every night from 9pm until midnight followed by a DJ until 2am with lots of activity on the large dance floor. Wednesday is AfroCuban night.

Patio del Decimista
Salvador Cisneros 112 A; tel: 48-796 014.
Live music in the courtyard from 5.30pm, then in the inner patio from 9pm until late. Very popular with locals and visitors, everyone gets up to dance and there are even some professional dancers to encourage participation.

Cienfuegos

Centro Nocturno Artex (Patio de Artex)
Calle 35 e/. 16 y 18, Punta Gorda; tel: 43-551 255.

Live music outside the Casa de la Música, Trinidad

This is the most important venue for musical events, hosting festivals and competitions as well as nightly live entertainment until 2am.

Club El Benny

Avenida 54 No 2907, Calles 27 y 29; tel: 43-451 105.

A smart 1950s-style nightclub named after local hero Benny Moré, with live entertainment: comedy, karaoke, bolero, and lots of dancing. Open from 9pm until late, show at 11pm, closed Sun.

Trinidad

Bar Yesterday (Casa de los Beatles)

Gustavo Izquierdo e/. Simón Bolívar y Piro Guinart.

Unmistakable because of the statues of John, Paul, George, and Ringo at the door to the bar, tribute bands play Beatles songs here but also other rock in English. Open 4pm–midnight.

Casa de la Música

On the steps up from the Plaza Mayor, tel: 41-996 622.

Music and dancing till the early hours. There's a restaurant, show 10pm–2am, piano bar open 6pm–6am and music shop, very popular with local people and visitors.

Las Cuevas

Finca Santa Ana; tel: 41-996 133.

This is in a hotel uphill from town, with the unusual setting of being in a cave below the reception. Dance among the stalactites from 10.30pm, very popular with Trinidadians as well as visitors.

Santa Clara

El Mejunje

Marta Abreu 107 e/. Alemán y Juan Bruno Zayas; tel: 42-282 572.

This is the place to be in Santa Clara. An outdoor venue in the shell of a building, with trees growing inside it, a small art gallery upstairs (indoors) and several bars, the walls are covered in graffiti. There is something different every night to suit all strands of society (jazz, rock, trova, golden oldies) but the stand-out night is LGBT Saturday when there is a transvestite show, popular with straight people too. Friday night the place fills up with university students, who spill out onto the road.

Camagüey

Casa de la Trova Patricio Ballagas

Cisneros e/. Martí y Cristo, on the west side of Parque Agramonte.

Folk and traditional music is played in the courtyard and there is a bar and music shop. Closed Mon and Sun night. Other days it is open 9am–7pm, then from 8.30pm to midnight Tue–Thu and till 2am Fri–Sat.

Santiago de Cuba

Casa de la Trova

Heredia 208 e/. San Pedro y San Félix; tel: 22-623 943

One of the best known *casas* in Cuba. Famous musicians play here and you

Dancing to the rhythm at the Casa de La Trova, Santiago

can hear *trova*, *son* and *boleros*. There is always something going on and most of it is excellent. Open Tue–Sun, day and night.

Casa de las Tradiciones, La Casona

Rabí 154 e/. José de Diego y García; tel: 22-653 892.

Smaller and more intimate than the Casa de la Trova, in a large colonial house with a central patio. Daytime concerts in the late morning and mid-afternoon are held downstairs, while there is a great upstairs dance floor and lounge known as the Salón de los Grandes. At night live *trova*,

Enjoying a drink at El Patio de Artex

son and *boleros* can be heard from 8pm. All the big names in Santiago play here.

El Patio de Artex

Heredia 304 e/. Carnicería y Calvario; tel: 22-654 814.

In the patio behind the Artex store there is often excellent live music with late-afternoon and evening sets. Dance or just have a drink and enjoy the music until 2am. The program changes daily but you can usually hear a *son* band at 5pm and something more contemporary at 9pm.

Teatro Heredia

Avenida de los Desfiles.

Outside the theatre there is a large open air space known as Pista Pacho Alonso, which is where concerts are held for top bands playing salsa, rap or *son*, although it is sometimes used as a large disco with a DJ. Inside the theatre is the Café Cantante, where you can hear live traditional music Fri–Sun at 9pm. It can get crowded when the best bands are playing.

Baracoa

El Ranchón

Loma Paraíso, above Calixto García; tel: 21-643 268.

This is the local disco, open air and with a great view over the town, but quite a climb up and down lots of steps. Live bands play here as well as DJs and, although it opens at 9pm, it doesn't really get going until midnight when the Casa de la Trova and Casa de la Música close. Popular with young Baracoans.

The Cuban flag

A–Z

A

Addresses

Addresses are easy to understand once you know a couple of the short-hands used: *C/.* = Street (*Calle* in Spanish); *Ave.* = Avenue (*Avenida*); *e/.* or *%* = between (*entre*); *esq.* or *esq. a* = on the corner of (*esquina*). In some areas, streets and avenues are named with numbers. Hence Calle 3 e/. 12 y Malecón is 3rd Street, between 12th Avenue and the Malecón. San Ignacio esq. Muralla is the corners of San Ignacio and Muralla Streets.

Admission charge

There is an admission charge for most museums, galleries, and other places of touristic interest. It is generally CUC$1–5. In many places, you pay extra if you are going to use a camera, and quite a lot extra to use a video camera.

Age restrictions

The age of consent is 18 in Cuba. Sex tourism is rife and foreign men are often seen in the company of young girls but this is illegal and can be a blackmail trap.

The minimum age for hiring a car is 21, although for some types of car the limit rises to 25.

B

Budgeting for your trip

A good hotel in Havana will cost around CUC$160 for a double room in high season. You can choose to stay in *casas particulares*, where you will, on average, be charged CUC$30–35 (less outside Havana), with breakfast costing around CUC$5 and dinner around CUC$10, depending on your menu choice.

Eating out is rarely very expensive, about CUC$25 per person in a smartish restaurant, but there are many restaurants and *paladares* where you can eat well for around CUC$15 or less. If you are going to drink wine, this puts the price up quite a lot. In a bar, beer costs around CUC$1.50, mojitos CUC$3–6, depending on location.

If you go to a town such as Bayamo, where you can pay in pesos Cubanos, food and drink will be much cheaper.

Car rental is expensive, around CUC$50 a day. Taxi fares are reasonable: you can get to most places in Havana for CUC$5 while a taxi to the airport from Old Havana is CUC$25. Long-distance bus fares are also reasonable; the longest journey you could make would be Havana to Santiago, which would currently set you back CUC$51.

Santiago snapshot

C

Children

Children will be pampered guests at any hotel and the employees will quickly learn their names and interests. The beach resorts all have supervised activities for them, and family rates are offered during the low season.

Clothing

Casual, comfortable clothes are appropriate anywhere on the island, especially light cotton garments that can be put on and taken off in layers as the temperature changes. Shorts and bathing suits are accepted at all seaside resorts, though more coverage is expected for dining out or visiting museums and galleries. Unless you're coming here for business you won't have much use for a suit and tie or a formal dress. A waterproof jacket is optional. Cubans often carry umbrellas for protection from the sun, and also whip them open at the first drop of rain.

Take comfortable walking shoes, a hat and dark glasses. If you are going to be traveling on long-distance buses bring a fleece or warm jersey. The air conditioning usually has only one setting in Cuba – high.

Crime and safety

Crime is still low by Latin American standards. Indeed, in comparison with most of the countries from which they come, visitors will find Cuba reassuringly safe. However, bag snatching and pickpocketing are not uncommon, particularly in the poorer sections of Havana and Santiago. Leave travel documents, large banknotes, and ostentatious jewelry in your hotel, and keep a firm grip on your camera and on any bag you decide to carry – bags are best worn crossed over your shoulder. Be sensible and take the same precautions you would in any large, unfamiliar city, and at night keep to busy and well-lit streets (or walk in the middle of the road if there is no street lighting). There is much less crime outside the capital, but in Santiago you must take the same precautions as you would in Havana.

Lost property

In case of theft, you should immediately report the crime to the nearest police station. Make sure you ask for the case report *(denuncia)* to back up any insurance claim on your return home. This may take time, but is essential if you intend to make a claim. The Cuban firm **Asistur** (tel: 7-866 8339 24 hours, www. asistur.cu) can help with cash advances and replacement of documents.

You should report lost or stolen passports to your embassy or consulate, which can issue emergency papers to get you home.

Customs regulations

Tourists may bring in, duty-free, personal effects (including up to 10 kg

Musicians in Baracoa

of medicine in its original packaging but it must be kept separate from the rest of your luggage) for their own use. Visitors can also bring in one carton of cigarettes and two bottles of alcoholic drinks. You may not bring in fruit or vegetables.

On departure you may take out 50 cigars as long as they are in their original packaging, unopened and sealed with the official hologram, or up to CUC$5,000-worth of cigars if, in addition, you have a formal sales invoice from the store where they were bought. Only 20 cigars can be taken out if you have no receipt or they are unsealed. You can take out up to six bottles of rum. Cash of up to US$5,000 (or equivalent) may be taken out of the country; any amount exceeding that must have been declared on arrival.

Further details on customs regulations can be found at www.aduana.gob.cu.

D

Disabled travelers

Travelers with disabilities may find getting around Cuba quite difficult. Most modern hotels and many refurbished hotels have facilities, but older hotels and other buildings do not. Streets and sidewalks are narrow, with storm drains, and wheelchair ramps do not exist. Public toilets (and those in restaurants and bars) are not adapted for people with disabilities.

E

Electricity

Both 220 and 110 volts are used, but 220 is more common. Electric outlets usually take plugs with two flat prongs, but you may find some that take round prongs. It's best to come prepared with adaptors and transformers so as not to be caught out. Power cuts are common.

Embassies and consulates

Canada: Calle 30, 518, corner of 7ma, Miramar, tel: (7) 204-2516.
Germany: Calle 13, 652, corner of B, Vedado, tel: (7) 833-2539, 833-2569.
Italy: Avenida 5, 402, corner of 4, Miramar, tel: (7) 204-5615.
Spain: Cárcel 51, corner Zulueta, Habana Vieja, tel: (7) 866-8025.
UK: Calle 34, 702, corner of 7, Miramar, tel: (7) 214-2200.
United States: Calzada, between L and M, Vedado, tel: (7) 839-4100.

For others, see http://embassy.go abroad.com.

Emergencies

106 for police, **105** for fire, **104** for ambulance.

Etiquette

Cuba is hot and many women wear skimpy tops, but bathing suits are for the beach and should not be worn around town. Dress decently to go into a

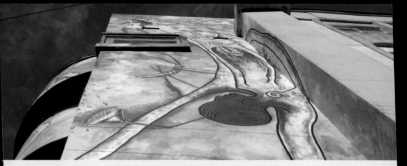

church or temple. There are often dress codes at nightclubs: Cubans dress smartly to go out at night and men are expected to wear long trousers and shirts with sleeves.

F

Festivals

All Cuban provinces celebrate a Culture Week *(Semana Cultural)* once a year, with music, dance, arts and crafts, and local food.

The Havana International Jazz Festival (http://jazzcuba.com) is held in January and is based in the Teatro Nacional de Cuba, the Teatro Amadeo Roldán, and Teatro Karl Marx; there are also impromptu performances elsewhere.

The International Film Festival (http://habanafilmfestival.com) is in December. Other festivals include the Havana Contemporary Music Festival in November, the International Ballet Festival in October, and the Havana Theater Festival in October.

Havana's carnival takes place in August with flamboyant parades on the Malecón throughout the day and night. Santiago de Cuba holds an even better carnival in late July.

A less well-known festival, wild and colorful Las Parrandas takes place in certain towns and villages of Villa Clara province, in the week between Christmas and New Year – most famously at Remedios.

G

Gay and lesbian travelers

The hardline Cuban policy on homosexuals has lessened in recent years (sex between consenting adults was legalized in 1979) and there is generally a more tolerant attitude. It is still not the most gay-friendly place to visit, although there is a growing number of openly gay people – mostly in the capital and in some small, laid-back places such as Viñales and Baracoa.

H

Health and medical care

No health certificate is required of visitors unless they are arriving from areas where cholera, smallpox, or yellow fever exist, in which case they must show a certificate of vaccination against those diseases. However, it's a good idea to be up to date with tetanus, typhoid, and hepatitis A vaccinations. There are no malarial areas in Cuba, but dengue fever, although it has been virtually eradicated through determined fumigation measures, may still occur. There is no vaccination, so do all you can to prevent mosquito bites – use a DEET-based repellent, and cover up in areas where mosquitoes are prevalent. The fever is spread by the *Aedes aegypti* mosquito which, unusually, tends to bite during the day rather than at night. The illness presents with flu-like symptoms and,

Mural in Varadero

while usually mild, can be serious.

You should bring all your own prescription drugs and common remedies such as aspirin with you. In Havana, the Farmacia Internacional is at Avenida 41 esq 20, Playa, tel: 7-204 2051. There are other good pharmacies at the Camilo Cienfuegos Hospital, Línea y Calle 13, Vedado, tel: 7-833 3599, and at the Clínica Central Cira García, Avenida 20 4101 esq 41, Playa, tel: 7-204 2880, open 24 hours. Outside Havana, try the international clinics in resort areas or any high-street pharmacy in urban areas.

To avoid upset stomachs and diarrhoea – the two main complaints suffered by tourists – drink bottled water – and plenty of it – and eat lightly. Be sensible about over exposure to the sun.

Medical services

All hotels have a first-aid post of sorts, and the larger hotels will have a resident doctor or nurse. Unless you fall ill in a remote rural area, as a foreign visitor you will be treated in a CUC-only hospital or a special tourist clinic (run by Servimed, www.servimedcuba.com).

Health insurance

Health insurance is mandatory for all visitors to Cuba. Tourists and all non-resident Cubans must hold a medical insurance policy (which includes repatriation for medical emergencies) issued by one of the specific companies approved by the Cuban government. If you do not have the correct papers, you will be forced to buy an approved insurance policy on arrival at the airport in Cuba.

Hours and holidays

Most banks open Mon–Fri 8.30am–3pm. Most Cuban offices open around 8.30am–5 or 6pm, often with a break at lunch time.

Farmers' markets open early, from around 7am or even earlier, and close when traders decide to leave – usually between 4 and 6pm.

CUC retail stores (often referred to as dollar stores) are all over Cuba; most open Mon–Sat 10am–5pm but may stay open later.

CUC supermarkets usually open Mon–Sat 9am–6pm and Sun 9am–1pm. Many of the bigger stores open 9am–9pm.

Public holidays

January 1 Liberation Day, commemorating the guerrillas' triumph over Batista.

May 1 Labor Day, celebrated with workers' parades.

July 25–27 A three-day holiday celebrating July 26, 1953, the date of the attack on the Moncada Garrison in Santiago, recognized as the start of the revolution.

October 10 Celebrating the start of the War of Independence against Spain in 1868.

December 25 Christmas Day.

In addition to these official public holidays, there are innumerable other important dates which are commemorated, including:

January 28 The birth of José Martí (1853).

Camagüey streetlife

April 19 The victory at the Bay of Pigs (1962).
Second Sunday in May Mother's Day
October 8 Death of Che Guevara.

Internet

Internet access is improving but very few Cubans have it at home. Tourist hotels have internet access and in some it is available to non-guests on presentation of a passport. This can be expensive, with the business centers in the top hotels charging up to CUC$15 per hour. Wi-Fi is rarely available in hotel rooms and you may have to use it in reception. Most towns have a branch of ETECSA (the telephone and communications company), which offers internet facilities and computers. You buy a card from ETECSA with a code for access to the internet for your phone or laptop. Wi-Fi hotspots are now common in most town plazas, identifiable by groups of Cubans on their phones. A few *casas particulares* now have Wi-Fi.

Language

Cubans speak Spanish. Most people working in the tourist industry speak English and other European languages, while some speak Russian and occasionally Chinese. Medical staff who have served abroad on brigades or disaster relief also speak English. See our language section, page 134.

Media

Newspapers and magazines

The printed media of Cuba is extremely limited due to paper shortages and governmental control. The only daily paper is the Communist Party organ, *Granma*, which mainly offers an update on solidarity, trade and agriculture, and provides interesting rather than scintillating reading. It is published weekly in Spanish, English, French, German, and Portuguese.

Four- and five-star hotels (particularly in Havana) often carry foreign publications from *Time* to *Cosmopolitan*.

Television

Cuban national television is broadcast on five state-owned national channels (Cubavisión, Tele Rebelde, Multivisión, Canal Educativo, and Canal Educativo 2). Foreign movies (usually American) are shown on Thursday, Friday, Saturday, and Sunday. Soaps, usually Brazilian, Colombian, Mexican, or Cuban, are extremely popular. North American soaps and series are also screened.

Tourist hotels all have satellite TV with more than 20 channels.

Radio

Just about everybody in Cuba has a radio, and loud music is a constant background sound wherever you go. There are six state-owned national radio stations and each province has its own station as well.

Cuban pesos

Radio Reloj (Clock Radio) gives round-the-clock news on AM, to the infuriating background noise of a ticking clock; Radio Havana Cuba broadcasts news and features on short wave, where the BBC also comes through, though the reception is poor.

Voice of America broadcasts from 6pm on 7070, short wave. Radio Martí, Voice of America's Spanish-language propaganda service, broadcasts from Miami, and often changes its frequencies to avoid jamming, but without much success.

Money

Currency

Although President Raúl Castro has announced his intention to unify the currency, at the moment Cuba still has two currencies: the *peso Cubano* (CUP or *moneda nacional*) divided into 100 centavos, and the *peso convertible* (CUC). Foreigners are expected to use CUC most of the time and will be charged in CUC for all accommodations, most food, and transportation. Euros can be used in the large resorts: Varadero, Cayo Largo, Cayo Coco, and Santa Lucía.

Some people find it useful to change a small amount of foreign currency into Cuban pesos (CUC\$1 = CUP24) for use on local buses, in cinemas, when shopping for fresh fruit at farmers' markets, when buying food and drink from street vendors, and in some off-the-beaten-track restaurants.

Changing money

You can change foreign currency into *pesos convertibles* at *cadeca* booths and some large banks. In Old Havana, *cadecas* can be found on Calle Obispo and Calle Oficios and elsewhere, and in Vedado there is one on La Rampa (Calle 23) and one on the corner of the Malecón and Calle D. Every sizable town has at least one. *Cadecas* change traveler's checks but you must produce the original purchase receipt as well as your passport. American Express traveler's checks or any others issued by a US bank are not accepted. British banks will not even sell you traveler's checks for use in Cuba for that reason.

Change some foreign currency into convertible pesos at the *cadeca* booth at the airport when you arrive. Bring sterling or euros if possible, as a 10 percent tax is charged on US dollars. Make sure your notes are clean, with no writing on them, as any blemished foreign currency will be rejected. Remember to keep enough convertible pesos to pay the CUC\$25 departure tax, but don't take them home with you except as souvenirs, since they are not, in fact, convertible currency, despite the name.

For the latest exchange rate that you will be charged in Cuba, see www.banco-metropolitano.com.cu.

Credit cards

Access/MasterCard, Visa, and other credit cards are welcome at most hotels, and some restaurants and stores, pro-

CAJA DE CAMBIOS
Currency Exchange

Currency exchange in Havana

vided they have been issued outside the US by non-US banks. The centralized computer system often fails, going down for hours at a time; this affects every credit-card machine in the land, and you will not be able to use your card at all while the system failure lasts.

If you need cash in an emergency, cash can be withdrawn against a credit card at branches of the Banco Financiero Internacional, and at *cadeca*, but all purchases of cash or goods on a credit card will be converted from CUCs to US dollars, incurring the 10 percent exchange tax, before conversion to your own currency by your credit card company, which may charge you further fees and commissions. There are ATMs in Havana – for example, at the *cadeca* office in Calle Obispo, available when the office itself is closed – each site should give the location of others in the area.

Cash

Always try to have a good supply of cash with you, particularly if you head out of Havana. Getting change from big bills is often difficult, so it is worthwhile keeping a stock of 10s, 5s, and single notes in your wallet. You will normally have to show your passport if you produce a 50- or 100-CUC bill in a Cuban store.

Be careful, when you pay for something, that the change you are given is in CUCs not *pesos cubanos* – the notes look extremely similar.

P

Post

Every rural town has a post office, and major cities have a central post office with municipal branches. You can buy stamps *(sellos)* here for pesos. In hotels, you will be charged the same price, but in CUCs. Some stamps are not glued, so you have to ask for a dab of glue at a post office.

Postcards and letters to Europe cost 75 cents. Delivery is slow. Postcards and letters to Europe and the Americas sometimes take a month or more.

R

Religion

The government blunted the influence of the Catholic Church in the early 1960s, but never cracked down on it completely. Since the Pope's visits to Cuba in 1998 and subsequently, there has been a relaxation of hostility from the government. Christmas is now widely celebrated and Christmas Day is a public holiday. Mass is still said in churches throughout the island.

In Havana, times of Mass in the cathedral in Old Havana are posted at the entrance. The Jewish synagogue at Línea y M holds services and has a library. The Methodist church, a block away from the Habana Libre Hotel at Calles 25 y K, lays on social activities as well as services, and has a small guest-

Phone box in Santiago

house. Abdallah mosque was opened in Old Havana in 2015, at Oficios 18; there is a Greek Orthodox church beside Plaza San Francisco and a Russian Orthodox cathedral on San Pedro 309 esq Santa Clara in Old Havana.

S

Smoking

Tobacco has been grown and smoked in Cuba since before the arrival of the Spanish and cigars remain one of the country's leading exports as well as being a major tourist attraction. However, attitudes to smoking have changed in line with the rest of the world and it is banned in most workplaces, indoor restaurants, and bars.

T

Telephones

The Cuban local telephone service has undergone a complete overhaul and it is now possible to make crackle-free calls right across the island (sometimes). The state telecommunications company, ETECSA, also known as Telepunto in some places, offers a full range of services, including phone rental, internet, and international calls.

Most public phones take pre-paid phonecards *(tarjetas)*. There are two types of card on offer: "chip" and "propia," which cost the same but the latter has cheaper rates at night and can be used to make calls from a private phone as well as a public call box. The best and cheapest cards to get are the Propia cards priced in *pesos cubanos*, but these are supposed to be reserved for Cubans and are difficult for tourists to get hold of. Foreigners are supposed to buy those priced in CUCs, which are extremely expensive. Propia cards give you a personal code which you input before using a phone. They can be bought at branches of ETECSA and cost 5 or 10 *pesos cubanos*.

Peso convertible cards, for local or international calls, can also be bought at ETECSA offices and at hotel reception desks, and come in denominations of 5, 10, 15, or 25 CUCs. Local calls cost about 5 *centavos* a minute, calls to other provinces cost about 35 *centavos* a minute. International calls with a Propia card are expensive: CUC$1.95 a minute to the US and Canada; CUC$3.65 a minute to Europe and the rest of the world (and even more if you call from a hotel), but there are reductions for calls between 6pm and 6am.

Collect calls (reverse charge/*cobro revertido*) can be made from a regular Cuban line (as found in most homes) to the US, Canada, the UK, Mexico, Puerto Rico, Portugal, Spain, and Italy, but they are prohibitively expensive. You cannot make a collect call from a hotel or a public phone.

It is possible to hire cell phones (mobiles) at Cubacel. There is an office of Cubacel at Telepunto, Calle Habana 406 e/. Obispo y Obrapía, in Old Havana, or they can be found in Etecsa offices

The romantically named Romeo and Julieta cigars

around the country. The head office is at Centro de Negocios Miramar, Edificio Santa Clara, 3 esq 78, tel: 5264 2266; www.etecsa.cu; and there is an office at Havana airport. Phones cost around CUC$5 a day to hire. Call charges are high, about 70 cents a minute for local calls, rising steeply for calls outside Cuba. As with your own cell phone if used abroad, you pay for incoming as well as outgoing calls, although an incoming call from abroad is free. The bill must be paid by cash or credit card. A deposit is refunded when the phone is returned and the bill has been paid. You can use your own cell phone in Cuba (where there is a signal) and sending a short text message home can be quicker and easier than struggling with the internet at Etecsa. Tariffs depend on your own service provider.

Telephone codes

Telephone numbers are usually six digits, except in Havana, where they are seven digits, and cell phones, which have eight digits (beginning with a 5).

If you're phoning from outside Cuba, dial the country code (53), then the area code, and then the number. Area codes are: Havana city 7, Havana province 47, Cienfuegos 43, Las Tunas 31, Pinar del Río 48, Villa Clara 42, Holguín 24, Sancti Spíritus 41 (except Condado, El Pedrero, Topes de Collantes 42), Granma 23, Isla de la Juventud 46, Cayo Largo del Sur 45, Ciego de Avila 33, Santiago de Cuba 22, Matanzas 45, Camagüey 32, and Guantánamo 21. No area code is needed

if you are dialling a cell/mobile phone.

Inside Cuba, to call another city from Havana you must dial 0 before the area code (eg Santa Clara from Havana 042-); to call Havana from another city you must dial 0 before the area code (07-); to call any city from another (eg Santa Clara from Cienfuegos) you must dial 01 before the area code (0142-). The 0 and 01 still apply if you are calling a cell/mobile phone; the initial 5 acts as an area code.

In general, don't use the area code when phoning within a province.

In listings in this guide we have not included the international code (53), and we have kept to the general rules outlined above, but be aware that there may be differences and changes.

To make an international call, first dial the access code 119, then the country code, area code, and phone number. International operators speak English.

Time zone

Cuba is on Eastern Standard Time (Daylight Saving applies during summer), which is GMT -5. When it's noon in Havana, it's 5pm in London, 6pm in Madrid and Rome, and 2pm in Buenos Aires.

Tipping

Taxi drivers, waiters, and hotel staff should be tipped in CUCs – this is the only access to convertible currency that they get. Ten percent is usual for taxi drivers and restaurant staff. You should leave CUC$1 a day for a hotel chambermaid.

Casa particular in Camagüey

Toilets

The first thing to remember about toilets is that Cuban plumbing is dodgy so you must always throw paper in the bin provided, not into the bowl – even in hotels with smart new facilities. The second thing is to take your own toilet paper with you on day trips. There are very few public restrooms and those that do exist (at bus stations, for example) charge for a few sheets of paper.

Tourist information

All hotels have a tourism bureau, where restaurant reservations can be made, sightseeing tours booked, etc. If you are staying in a *casa particular*, the owners will be a good source of information.

General tourist information offices do not really exist in Cuba. Infotur is the only tourist-information service, with kiosks at José Martí Airport, Terminal 3 (tel: 7-642 6101; in Old Havana at Calle Obispo 521 e/. Bernaza y Villegas (tel: 7-866 3333), and out in Playas del Este at Avenida Las Terrazas e/. 11 and 12, Santa María del Mar (tel: 7-797 1261).

Tours and guides

There is a whole range of state tourism enterprises whose services sometimes overlap and which concentrate on offering packages or other specific services, but they can give assistance in all areas, and most of them have improved greatly in recent years in both helpfulness and efficiency. There are also a growing number of private guides offering tours, although you usually have to provide the transport. Your casa particular owner will be able to put you in touch with a private operator.

Amistur Cuba specializes in people-to-people tours, or political tours for people wishing to see the revolutionary side of Cuba. They can be found on Paseo 406 e/. 17 y 19, Vedado, tel: 7-830 1220, 7-833 4544; www.amistur.cu.

Cubatur sells excursions through the tourism bureaux in most of Cuba's hotels and in their own offices, which can be found in most towns and resorts; in Havana at Calle F 157 e/. 9 y Calzada, Vedado, tel: 7-835 4115; www.cubatur.cu.

Ecotur is the agency which deals with nature tourism, http://cubanaturetravel.com or www.ecoturcuba.tur.cu, including birdwatching and hiking.

Gaviota books hotel accommodations, organizes excursions, car rental, dive packages, and more; Edificio La Marina, 3rd floor, Avenida del Puerto 102, Old Havana, tel: 7-204 7683; www.gaviota-grupo.com.

Havanatur arranges hotel accommodations, as well as excursions of all kinds. It has its own fleet of buses and a car rental agency, Havanautos. Its headquarters are in the Edificio Sierra Maestra, Calle 1 e/. 2 y 0, Miramar, tel: 7-830 8227; www.havanatur.cu.

Transport

Arrival by air

The availability of flights to Cuba and the airlines in service are subject to change

José Martí airport, Havana

and vary according to season, so always check. There are international airports at Havana, Varadero, Holguín, Santiago de Cuba, Ciego de Avila, Cayo Coco, Cayo Largo, Santa Clara, Las Tunas, Manzanillo, and Camagüey. *Cubana de Aviación*, the national airline, flies scheduled and charter routes between Cuba and other cities in the Americas and Europe, serving primarily Havana, but also Holguín, Santa Clara, Camagüey, and Santiago de Cuba. Most flights are positively no-frills, but Cubana flights provide the cheapest route into Cuba.

From Europe

Cubana (www.cubana.cu) flies from: Paris, Moscow, Madrid, and Rome.

Air France (www.airfrance.com) has scheduled flights to Havana from Paris; there are good connections from other European cities.

Iberia (www.iberia.com) and Air Europa (www.aireuropa.com) operate scheduled flights from Madrid with connections from London and other European cities.

KLM (www.klm.com) flies from Amsterdam with connections from British and mainland European cities.

Virgin (www.virgin-atlantic.com) operates direct flights from Gatwick to Havana.

There are charter flights from Amsterdam and airports in the UK to Havana, Varadero, and Holguín, usually booked through package-tour operators.

From Latin America and the Caribbean

Cubana flies to and from: Bogotá, Buenos Aires, Cancún, Fort-de-France, Managua, Mexico City, Nassau, Pointe-à-Pitre, Port-au-Prince, San José, and Santo Domingo.

AeroGaviota flies from Kingston, Jamaica to Havana via Santiago and from Montego Bay to Havana via Holguín.

Many Latin American and Caribbean airlines also serve Cuba, with scheduled and charter flights available. **Mexicana** (www.mexicana.com) flies between Mexico City and Havana, and there are also frequent flights from Cancún and Mérida in Yucatán. There are regular connections between Havana and various Central American cities with local airlines (www.grupotaca.com).

From Canada

Cuba is accessible by air from Montreal and Toronto. **Cubana** runs scheduled flights from Montreal and Toronto, while **Air Canada** (www.aircanada.ca) flies from Toronto to Havana, Varadero, Santa Clara, Holguín, Cayo Coco, and Ciego de Avila. Direct flight time from Montreal to Havana is 4 hours; 3 hours 45 minutes from Toronto. There are also charter flights from Ottawa.

From the US

In 2015, restrictions on US citizens visiting Cuba were relaxed, allowing 12 categories of travel. Scheduled flights are now operating (in addition to charters) taking US travelers to Cuba, mostly on people-to-people programs, or Cuban Americans visiting relatives. American Airlines, Jet Blue, Delta, Southwest, and Sun Country are the main carriers, flying from Miami, Atlanta, Chicago, Philadelphia, Minneapolis, and Fort Lauderdale.

Taxis in Trinidad

On Departure

Allow at least 45 minutes for the trip from Old Havana to the airport. Be at the airport at least 2 hours before an international flight; security and customs checks can be lengthy.

Airport departure tax for international flights is CUC$25, which must be paid after you have checked in, in cash, in *pesos convertibles*.

By sea

There are over 20 marinas and nautical centers for people traveling on chartered (or private) yachts. There is no ferry service. Some cruise lines stop in Cuba, ships dock in Havana, in Cienfuegos, or in Santiago de Cuba.

Getting around

Cuba is a long, thin island, about the length of England, and distances between towns can be greater than expected. All transport radiates from the Havana hub. There are road and rail links between Havana and Pinar del Río in the west and Havana and Santiago de Cuba in the east, while many towns are also connected with Havana by air.

From Havana Airport

José Martí International Airport, tel: 7-649 5666 for international flight information; 7-266 4133 for domestic flights. Most international flights operate from Terminal 3, where there is a tourist information desk, numerous car-rental desks, bars, restaurants, and an exchange desk.

Some charter flights use Terminal 2.

Taxis are always available: the fare is around CUC$25 to the old city, although you may be charged as little as CUC$15 on the return. (The airport is about 11 miles/ 18 km from central Havana.) Drivers gather at the terminal and hustle for your custom. It is illegal for unlicensed cabs to drive tourists to or from the airport.

By air

Most services originate from Havana. The national airline, **Cubana** (www.cubana.cu), has regular scheduled flights to 13 Cuban cities from the capital.

Aerogaviota operate flights to Cayo Largo, Cayo Coco, Cayo Santa María, and other popular destinations from a separate, small airport near Havana at Baracoa Beach, Carretera Panamericana Km 15.5, Caimito, Artemisa, tel: 7-209 8002 for airport information.

Purchase tickets for domestic flights from a hotel reception desk or a recognised travel agency. They do not charge commission for making the airline booking.

By bus

City buses, known as *guaguas*, are crowded and uncomfortable, but they are cheap (take care of your valuables). They are motorized in Havana and Santiago de Cuba, but in many cities they are horse-drawn and foreigners are not encouraged to use them. A hop-on, hop-off bus service for tourists is in operation in Havana, called the HabanaBusTour, with

Buses in Havana

two routes, one from the Almacenes San José on Av del Puerto to Vedado, Plaza de la Revolución and Miramar (CUC$10 per day) and the other from the Parque Central out to Playas del Este via the Castillo del Morro (CUC$5). A similar service runs from Varadero to Matanzas; from Trinidad to Playa Ancón and around Viñales.

Víazul is a CUC-only long-distance bus service offering fast, comfortable, air-conditioned vehicles and plenty of luggage capacity. The Víazul station is on Avenida 26 esq Zoológico, Nuevo Vedado, tel: 7-881 1413, www.viazul.com. Buy tickets in advance. You still have to turn up about 45 minutes in advance, but it's safer than lining up for a ticket without a reservation.

Some destinations such as Cienfuegos, Trinidad, Pinar del Río and Viñales can also be reached by transfer service with Transtur, which charges much the same price as Víazul. However, Transtur picks up passengers with reservations from hotels (not *casas particulares*) in the city, so you can save yourself the taxi fare out to the bus station. You book your seat through hotels' reservation desks. Departures are usually early in the morning, but vary according to demand.

By train

The Cuban railroad was the first in Latin America, but it may be the last in efficiency and comfort today. Trains are crowded and services have been reduced – almost all are now locals that stop at every station. All are achingly slow and

prone to breakdown. Little or no food or water is to be had, so take provisions with you, and a flashlight and toilet paper.

Seats on Cuban trains are always booked well in advance with long waiting lists, but there are always seats reserved for those paying in CUCs. Book your ticket a day in advance, and arrive at least an hour before departure to check in, and before 7pm if taking a night train: unassigned seats will be re-allocated if you have not confirmed that you are traveling.

In Havana buy your tickets in advance at agencies or the Estación La Coubre, from where all trains depart; Av del Puerto y Egido; tel: 7-860 3165; Mon-Fri 8.30am-4pm, Sat 8.30-11.30am. You must pay in CUCs, and bring your passport.

Driving

Renting a car gives the greatest degree of independence, and allows you to reach corners of the island that otherwise would be hard to get to. Highways and secondary roads are fairly well maintained, except for the potholes. Otherwise, driving is safe and Cubans are helpful with directions – though often vague when it comes to distances. There are very few road signs; a good map is essential; or be prepared to pick up hitchhikers who can direct you. Do not drive after dark; Cubans often drive with headlights on full beam and animals may wander onto the road. Away from cities, traffic congestion isn't a problem: you may travel miles without seeing another vehicle – even stretches of the *autopista* can be empty.

Private car in Santiago

In towns, traffic usually moves at the speed of bicycles and horses.

Car Rental

Current charges range between CUC$45 and CUC$100 per day, depending on the vehicle, plus a deposit of CUC$200–300. The fee and deposit must be paid in advance (cash or non-US credit card). Unlimited mileage is included but insurance and fuel are extra. The tank should be full when you start and you must return the car empty.

Super Collision Damage Waiver is compulsory. The cost depends on the make and size of the car but is around CUC$20 for a compact car.

Check the car carefully for damage and scratches. Draw attention to anything you find, and insist any damages are noted on the paperwork. Be sure to take out the maximum insurance cover possible; it is well worth the extra cost, in case of even minor scrapes or mishaps.

If you are involved in an accident or have something stolen from the car, report this to the police and get the right paperwork (*denuncia*) or you will not be able to claim insurance in Cuba or at home. The business at the police station will be time-consuming and may take many hours.

Cars can be rented through hotels or direct with the agencies. The main rental companies are Rex (www.rexcarrental.com), Cubacar, Havanautos, and Transtur (all on www.transtur.cu), and Vía Rent-a-Car (www.gaviota-grupo.com). They are all state-owned and there is little competition.

Gas (Petrol)

Cupet gas stations are found in all the main towns and, increasingly, in smaller provincial towns all over the island. Cupet stations normally offer minimal mechanical backup, as well as snack bars. Most are open 24 hours.

Private cars & taxis

Private taxis should be licensed. Some drivers charge a flat rate for a half or whole day of sightseeing or for a particular excursion, for example from Havana to Varadero or Havana to Viñales and back. Always agree a price before you set off.

There is only one taxi company: Cubataxi, tel: 7-855 5555 in Havana, which has been privatized with the cars leased to their (self-employed) drivers. You can call them or pick them up from designated ranks (usually outside hotels, and major museums). They are usually cheap, friendly, reliable, and metered (starting at CUC$1, then up to CUC$1 per kilometer, depending on the car). Peso taxis (colectivos) run on fixed routes, usually old, tatty cars which squeeze passengers in. They charge CUP10.

Coco-taxis

These are the little round, yellow, two-seater motorbike taxis that are fine (and fun) for short distances. They charge a minimum of CUC$3, and CUC$5–10 per hour.

Bicitaxis

These little rickshaw-type vehicles, drawn by bicycles, can be fun and are inexpensive – but agree a fare before you start, usually CUC$1–2 in town centers.

Coco taxis

Horse Carriages

In provincial towns horse-drawn wagons (called *coches*) provide an inexpensive bus service, and are widely used by local people. In tourist areas, such as Havana or Varadero, more luxurious carriages are available for sightseeing tours.

Cycling

Cycling is the way many Cubans get around, and you will have no trouble finding someone to mend a flat tire. There are cycle lanes on many roads outside towns. Bring a strong lock, and be careful where you park, or you may find yourself going home without your bicycle. Don't cycle in the middle of the day when the sun is at its height, nor after dark as roads are poorly lit and you may hit a cow.

V

Visas and passports

All visitors entering Cuba must show a passport valid for at least six months beyond the date of arrival in Cuba. In addition, visitors must have a **tourist card** (*tarjeta de turista*), issued by the Cuban Consulate directly or, more commonly, through a travel agent. This will be valid for the length of your planned visit, but can be extended (once) up to the date shown on your return airplane ticket – as long as the total time you are in the country does not exceed 60 days. Immigration officials stamp your tourist card, not your passport. Do not lose it – you

must show it when you leave the country.

Visas for US citizens

These are handled by the Cuban Embassy in Washington, DC. United States Treasury Department regulations prohibit US citizens from spending money in Cuba unless they qualify as journalists, researchers, businesspeople in specifically licensed sectors, or relatives of Cubans living on the island.

W

Weights and measures

Officially, Cuba uses the metric system, but you will find that goods at places that deal mostly with Cuban shoppers, such as farmers' markets, use imperial pounds (*libras*).

Women travelers

Cuba is not a difficult or dangerous place in which to travel as a single woman. Cubans out in the hinterland may regard a foreign woman traveling alone as unusual, but they will normally be friendly and helpful. Women are generally safer in Cuba than in most places in the world. Although rape is uncommon in Cuba, it does happen.

Women can expect a lot of male attention: this may be in the form of whistling, hissing, or comments. This can be annoying but it is rarely aggressive. Ignore the perpetrators and they will normally leave you alone. Any kind of acknowledgment is likely to be taken as a come-on.

Unity, strength, victory

LANGUAGE

Basic rules

Spanish is the language of Cuba. It is a phonetic language: words are pronounced exactly as they are spelled. Spanish distinguishes between the two genders, masculine and feminine. As a general rule, the accent falls on the second-to-last syllable, unless it is otherwise marked with an accent (´) or the word ends in D, L, R, or Z.

The following brief lexicon is Spanish as spoken in Spain, with a few Cuban amendments. A list of 'Cubanisms' follows.

Words and phrases

Hello *Hola*
How are you? *¿Cómo está usted?*
What is your name? *¿Cómo se llama usted?*
My name is... *Yo me llamo...*
Do you speak English? *¿Habla inglés?*
I am British/American *Yo soy británico(a)/norteamericano(a)*
I don't understand *No comprendo*
Can you help me? *¿Me puede ayudar?*
I am looking for... *Estoy buscando*
Where is...? *¿Dónde está...?*
I'm sorry *Lo siento/Perdone*
I don't know *No lo sé*
No problem *No hay problema*
There isn't any *No hay*
Have a good day *Que tenga un buen día*
Let's go *Vámonos*
See you tomorrow *Hasta mañana*
See you soon *Hasta pronto*
At what time? *¿A qué hora?*

When? *¿Cuándo?*
What time is it? *¿Qué hora es?*
yes/no *sí/no*
please *por favor*
thank you (very much) *(muchas) gracias*
you're welcome *de nada*
goodbye *adiós*
good evening/night *buenas tardes/noches*
today *hoy*
yesterday *ayer*
tomorrow *mañana* (note: *mañana* also means 'morning')
tomorrow morning *mañana por la mañana*
the day after tomorrow *pasado mañana*
now *ahora*
later *después*
this afternoon/evening *esta tarde*
tonight *esta noche*
next week *la semana que viene*

Getting around

I want to get off at... *Quiero bajarme en...*
Is there a bus to ...? *¿Hay un omnibús a ....?*
I'd like a taxi *Quisiera un taxi.*
Please take me to... *Por favor, lléveme a...*
How much will it cost? *¿Cuánto va a costar el viaje?*
Keep the change *Guarde el cambio.*
What street is this? *¿Qué calle es ésta?*
How far is...? *¿A qué distancia está...?*

Patriotic sign

airport *aeropuerto*
customs *aduana*
train station *estación de tren*
bus station *estación de omnibuses/ terminal de guaguas*
bus stop *parada de omnibús*
platform *andén*
ticket *tickete/boleto*
round-trip ticket *boleto de ida y vuelta*
hitchhiking *autostop/la botella*
restrooms/toilets *baños*
This is the hotel address *Ésta es la dirección del hotel*

Numbers

1 *uno*
2 *dos*
3 *tres*
4 *cuatro*
5 *cinco*
6 *seis*
7 *siete*
8 *ocho*
9 *nueve*
10 *diez*

Days of the week

Monday *lunes*
Tuesday *martes*
Wednesday *miércoles*
Thursday *jueves*
Friday *viernes*
Saturday *sábado*
Sunday *domingo*

Months

January *enero*
February *febrero*
March *marzo*
April *abril*
May *mayo*
June *junio*
July *julio*
August *agosto*
September *septiembre*
October *octubre*
November *noviembre*
December *diciembre*

Cuban expressions

Asere/chama **friend**
Consorte/yunta **close friend**
Jevo/a **boyfriend/girlfriend/young woman**
Mango young, **sexy man**
Chama/ambia **partner/friend**
Cundango/loca/pájaro **gay**
mamey **mummy (used casually to women of any age)**
Qué bola, asere! **What's up, man?**
Qué onda/hubo **Hi there!**
Cuál es la vuelta? **How's it going?**
Bárbaro/enpingao/encojonao/escapao **cool/great!**
Di tú! **Tell me about it!**
Aquí, en la lucha **You know how it is**
No es fácil **Things aren't easy**
Chao pesca'o **Bye, bye!**
Bueno, voy en pira **Right, I'm going now**
Eres un mangón **You're looking really good**
Fula/verde **Hard currency**
Gao **house/home**
Pincha **work**
Ser un luchador **to try any means to make money**

Wim Wenders' Buena Vista Social Club

BOOKS AND FILM

In the 19th century, Cuba's brightest star was poet and revolutionary, José Martí, who is honored in every town and village. Since then, the island has produced some outstanding writers.

After the Revolution, many exiled Cuban writers returned and there was a literary renaissance. However, the arrest of Herberto Padilla in 1968 for his poems discrediting the myths of revolutionary society triggered a crackdown on dissent. Many writers left and it was not until the 1990s that the exodus of writers and artists forced the government to take a more lenient attitude. Cuban writers now find it easier to express their ideas without heavy censorship, writing about the difficulties of making a living and openly critical of the sacrifices demanded by the state.

Film is the most favored of the arts. Cuban cinema kicked off with the arrival of Castro and the Cuban Institute of Cinematography (ICAIC), but after the heyday of the 1960s, economic constraints pushed the film industry to crisis point in the 1990s. Subsequent films have largely been made with the help of foreign finance.

The New Latin American Film Festival, held in Havana every December, attracts film-makers and actors from all over the world. Its prestigious Coral prizes are the Latin American equivalent of the Oscars. The International Low-Budget Film Festival, held in Gibara in April, showcases films that have cost less than US$300,000 to make.

Books

Non-Fiction

Before Night Falls: A Memoir by Reinaldo Arenas. A powerful memoir tracing the struggle of a young gay writer in Cuba at a time when there was no sexual or artistic freedom, his flight to New York, and his final battle with AIDS. Later made into a movie, starring Johnny Depp and Javier Bardem, this is one of the iconic books of the late 20th century.

Mea Cuba by Guillermo Cabrera Infante. Cabrera Infante chose exile after the Revolution and was a persistent critic of Fidel Castro. This collection of essays introduces the reader to Cuban writers, artists and other intellectuals who were ground down by the brutal regime if they dared to think independently.

Cuba: Or the Pursuit of Freedom by Hugh Thomas. A comprehensive and extensive history of Cuba; one of the most authoritative and informative.

Afrocuba, an Anthology of Cuban Writing on Race, Politics and Culture edited by Pedro Pérez Sarduy and Jean Stubbs. The relationship between Africa and Cuba is examined in essays on fiction, drama, poetry, history, and politics.

Salsa: Havana Heat, Bronx Beat by Hernando Calvo Ospina. The history of salsa is examined, from the slave ships to New York clubs, taking in *son*, jazz and cha cha chá as well as Colombian *cumbia* and the Dominican Republic's *merengue*.

Benicio del Toro in Che

Fiction

Dirty Havana Trilogy by Pedro Juan Gutiérrez, translated by Natasha Wimmer. The protagonist, Pedro Juan, explores himself and Havana through sex, drugs, rum, music, and other self-indulgences.

Dreaming in Cuban by Cristina García. Grandmother remains in Cuba, her daughter in the US, the granddaughter is visiting the matriarch. The three generations' relationships are complex, intertwined with the Cuban condition.

Our Man in Havana by Graham Greene. A black comedy set in the time of Batista. Wormold, a vacuum-cleaner salesman agrees to work as a British spy. His web of deceit becomes ever more convoluted as fiction and reality collide.

The Man Who Loved Dogs by Leonardo Padura Fuentes, translated by Anna Kushner. The man who killed Trotsky turns up secretly in Havana and meets a Cuban writer. A detective story with a difference, an indictment of Stalinism and a tale of politics, intrigue, and lost illusions.

Film

Memorias del Subdesarrollo (Memories of Underdevelopment), 1969. Tomás Gutiérrez Alea directed this classic movie about a middle-class Cuban who refuses to leave for Miami in the early 1960s but is unable to fit into revolutionary society.

Fresa y Chocolate (Strawberry and Chocolate), 1994. Gutiérrez Alea and Juan Carlos Tabío directed this Oscar-nominated film about a young Communist student and a gay intellectual, both fiercely patriotic, but the former identifies with Fidel and Che while the latter is hounded by the authorities and eventually seeks asylum abroad.

Buena Vista Social Club, 1998. Wim Wenders' documentary is a nostalgic reconstruction of the band of the same name, with Rubén González on piano, Ibrahim Ferrer on vocals and Ry Cooder on guitar, practising for two concerts in 1998. The film sparked a renaissance for the old style of Cuban music.

Suite Habana, 2003. This highly acclaimed documentary by Fernando Pérez Valdés chronicles a day in the life of several real people in Havana. Filmed without dialogue, it can be interpreted as critical and subversive or as a tribute to the resilience of people supporting the Revolution.

El Cuerno de la Abundancia (Horn of Plenty), 2008. Comedy directed by Juan Carlos Tabío, based on a true story of a family in a small town who hear they may have inherited a fortune in London. It follows their hopes and dreams, their struggles against bureaucracy, their greed and their fights, until they discover that the inheritance has gone to relatives in Miami.

Che Part 1: The Argentine; Che Part 2: The Guerrilla, 2008. This monumental biopic of Che, starring Benicio del Toro and directed by Steven Soderbergh, had to be filmed in Mexico and Puerto Rico because of the US embargo, but was shown to huge acclaim at the Latin American Film Festival. It follows Che through the Cuban Revolution and then his doomed attempt to export revolution to Bolivia.

ABOUT THIS BOOK

This *Explore Guide* has been produced by the editors of Insight Guides, whose books have set the standard for visual travel guides since 1970. With top-quality photography and authoritative recommendations, these guidebooks bring you the very best routes and itineraries in the world's most exciting destinations.

BEST ROUTES

The routes in the book provide something to suit all budgets, tastes and trip lengths. As well as covering the destination's many classic attractions, the itineraries track lesser-known sights. The routes embrace a range of interests, so whether you are an art fan, a gourmet, a history buff or have kids to entertain, you will find an option to suit.

We recommend reading the whole of a route before setting out. This should help you to familiarise yourself with it and enable you to plan where to stop for refreshments – options are shown in the 'Food and Drink' box at the end of each tour.

For our pick of the tours by theme, consult Recommended Routes for… (see pages 6–7).

INTRODUCTION

The routes are set in context by this introductory section, giving an overview of the destination to set the scene, plus background information on food and drink, shopping and more, while a succinct history timeline highlights the key events over the centuries.

DIRECTORY

Also supporting the routes is a Directory chapter, with a clearly organised A–Z of practical information, our pick of where to stay while you are there and select restaurant listings; these eateries complement the more low-key cafés and restaurants that feature within the routes and are intended to offer a wider choice for evening dining. Also included here are some nightlife listings and our recommendations for books and films about the destination.

ABOUT THE AUTHORS

Sarah Cameron has spent a lifetime traveling in Latin America and the Caribbean, working first as an economist and then as an author of travel guides. The Caribbean islands, and Cuba in particular, have become her specialty and she has contributed to many Insight Guides to the region.

CONTACT THE EDITORS

We hope you find this Explore Guide useful, interesting and a pleasure to read. If you have any questions or feedback on the text, pictures or maps, please do let us know. If you have noticed any errors or outdated facts, or have suggestions for places to include on the routes, we would be delighted to hear from you. Please drop us an email at hello@insightguides.com. Thanks!

CREDITS

Explore Cuba
Editor: Carine Tracanelli
Author: Sarah Cameron
Head of Production: Rebeka Davies
Update Production: Apa Digital
Picture Editor: Tom Smyth
Cartography: Carte
Photo credits: 123RF 22, 47MC; Alamy 24, 36, 67; Alejandro Ernesto/Epa/REX/Shutterstock 75T; Christian Kober/robertharding/REX/Shutterstock 116; Dreamstime 93L; Fabian von Poser/imageBROKER/REX/Shutterstock 86T; FLPA/Neil Bowman/REX/Shutterstock 51; Getty Images 23, 25L, 24/25, 26, 27, 66, 68, 73, 74, 74/75T, 112, 114B; Harry Laub/imageBROKER/REX/Shutterstock 84; iStock 1, 4MR, 6ML, 6BC, 14/15T, 28/29T, 37, 38/39, 44, 49, 68/69, 113; Jane Sweeney/AWL Images 4/5T, 8/9T, 98/99T; Kempinski Hotels 100; Meliá 102, 103; Patrick Frilet/REX/Shutterstock 106; Richard Isaac/REX/Shutterstock 114T, 117T; Road Movie Prods/Kobal/REX/Shutterstock 136; Shutterstock 4ML, 6MC, 8ML, 30, 46/47T, 50, 52/53, 69L, 70T, 71, 72, 75M, 77M, 85, 107, 109, 110; Sovfoto/Universal Images Group/REX/Shutterstock 86B; SuperStock 7M, 54, 76/77, 115; Sylvaine Poitau/Apa Publications 4MC, 4MR, 4MC, 4ML, 6TL, 7T, 7MR, 7MR, 8ML, 8MC, 8MC, 8MR, 8MR, 10, 11L, 10/11, 12B, 12T, 13, 14B, 16, 17L, 16/17, 18, 19, 20, 21M, 21T, 20/21T, 28ML, 28MC, 28MR, 28ML, 28MC, 28MR, 31L, 30/31, 32, 33, 34, 35L, 34/35, 40, 41L, 40/41, 42, 43L, 42/43, 45, 46, 47T, 48, 55, 56, 57L, 56/57, 58, 59L, 58/59, 60, 61, 62, 63L, 62/63, 64, 65L, 64/65, 78, 79B, 79T, 80, 81MC, 81T, 80/81T, 82B, 82T, 83, 87, 88, 89, 90, 91L, 90/91, 92, 92/93, 94, 95, 96, 97L, 96/97, 98ML, 98MC, 98MR, 98MR, 98MC, 98ML, 101, 104, 105, 108, 111, 117B, 118, 119, 120, 121, 122, 123, 124, 125, 126, 127, 128, 129, 130, 131, 132, 133, 134, 135; Valerio Berdini/REX/Shutterstock 70B; Wild Bunch/Morena/Kobal/REX/Shutterstock 137
Cover credits: iStock (main&bottom)

Printed by CTPS – China

DISTRIBUTION

UK, Ireland and Europe
Apa Publications (UK) Ltd
sales@insightguides.com
United States and Canada
Ingram Publisher Services
ips@ingramcontent.com
Australia and New Zealand
Woodslane
info@woodslane.com.au
Southeast Asia
Apa Publications (Singapore) Pte
singaporeoffice@insightguides.com
Worldwide
Apa Publications (UK) Ltd
sales@insightguides.com

SPECIAL SALES, CONTENT LICENSING AND COPUBLISHING

Insight Guides can be purchased in bulk quantities at discounted prices. We can create special editions, personalised jackets and corporate imprints tailored to your needs.
sales@insightguides.com
www.insightguides.biz

INDEX

MAP LEGEND

●	Start of tour
→	Tour & route direction
❶	Recommended sight
❷	Recommended restaurant/café
★	Place of interest
❶	Tourist information
✈	Airport
▭▭	Railway
·---	Ferry route
🚌	Main bus station
♁	Monument
ᴍ̂	Museum/gallery
✝	Church
✳	Viewpoint
◤	Beach
♌	Cave
☗	Lighthouse
--- •	National park, nature reserve
▭	Important building
▭	Park
▭	Urban area
▭	Non-urban area